Get That Job With NLP

Jackie Arnold

Dedication

*This book is dedicated to my mother
Pamela Alice Forsyth:*

*For her courage, humour and support
for me in everything I do.*

Jackie Arnold is an executive and leadership coach, who was on the Board of Directors of the UK International Coaching Federation from 2001–04. She holds a Diploma of Education, a Certificate in Business Coaching and an ICF Recognized Diploma in Coaching Supervision with the Coaching Supervision Academy.

Her career spans a number of interesting jobs, including BBC broadcaster, cruise ship entertainments officer, nursery school owner and manager in Switzerland, and lecturer and examinations writer for the LCCIEB. She has also set up English language schools in Switzerland and Poland.

Jackie is trained in NLP, Emotional Intelligence, Transactional Analysis, as well as a range of assessment tools; she is also a Clean Language coach and facilitator. Since 1998 she has owned and managed her own coaching and training business in the UK and Europe.

Get That Job With NLP

Jackie Arnold

First published in Great Britain in 2012 by Hodder & Stoughton. An Hachette UK company.

First published in US in 2012 by The McGraw-Hill Companies, Inc

This edition published 2012

Copyright © Jackie Arnold 2012

The right of Jackie Arnold to be identified as the Author of the Work has been asserted by her in accordance with the Copyright, Designs and Patents Act 1988.

Database right Hodder Education (makers)

The Teach Yourself name is a registered trademark of Hachette UK

British Library Cataloguing in Publication Data: a catalogue record for this title is available from the British Library.

Library of Congress Catalog Card Number: on file

10 9 8 7 6 5 4 3 2 1

The publisher has used its best endeavours to ensure that any website addresses referred to in this book are correct and active at the time of going to press. However, the publisher and the author have no responsibility for the websites and can make no guarantee that a site will remain live or that the content will remain relevant, decent or appropriate.

The publisher has made every effort to mark as such all words which it believes to be trademarks. The publisher should also like to make it clear that the presence of a word in the book, whether marked or unmarked, in no way affects its legal status as a trademark.

Every reasonable effort has been made by the publisher to trace the copyright holders of material in this book. Any errors or omissions should be notified in writing to the publisher, who will endeavour to rectify the situation for any reprints and future editions.

Cover image © gunnar3000 – Fotolia

Typeset by Cenveo Publisher Services.

Printed in Great Britain by CPI Group (UK) Ltd, Croydon.

Hodder & Stoughton policy is to use papers that are natural, renewable and recyclable products and made from wood grown in sustainable forests. The logging and manufacturing processes are expected to conform to the environmental regulations of the country of origin.

Hodder & Stoughton Ltd

338 Euston Road

London NW1 3BH

www.hodder.co.uk

Also available in ebook

Acknowledgements

Thanks to my cousin Lynn Flowers for her wonderful illustrations.

Case studies from:

Neil Williams, NLP Master Practitioner, Coach and Coach Supervisor

Steve Preston, Career Coach at The Career Catalyst

Chris Stribblehill, Clean Language Business Coach and Facilitator, at Coaching Made Simple

Thanks for expertise and contributions from:

Marian Way, Clean Coach and Facilitator at Clean Training

Judy Rees, co-author of *Clean Language* at X Ray Listening

Caitlin Walker, Clean Coach and Trainer at Training Attention Ltd

James Lawley and Penny Tompkins, authors of *Metaphors in Mind: Transformation of Symbolic Modelling,* who have been at the forefront of developing and promoting the application of Clean Language.

Lynne Burney, Executive Coach and Coach Supervisor

Members of EGG – European Growth Group

Brian Birch, Clean Practitioner

Allison Galbraith, Clean Corporate Coach at CleanComm

I would also like to thank:

My agent Fiona Spencer Thomas for her continued support.

My editors at Hodder & Stoughton for their guidance and patience.

My family and friends for their encouragement and gentle nudges when needed.

Contents

Foreword

Getting a job is one of the most important things in life. Whether your aim is to get *any* job, find the right job, or to take a step on your career path, there's always an element of luck involved. French scientist, Louis Pasteur, knew a thing or two about taking advantage of luck when he proclaimed, 'Chance favours the prepared mind'. And that is what *Get That Job With NLP* is all about, preparing yourself to be the best you can before, during and after the application and selection process. This much is in your own hands.

Whether you actually get the job depends on a host of other factors: your suitability for the role, the other candidates, the organization, managers and circumstances. You may not be able to control fate, destiny, karma or good fortune, but you can tip the balance. And that is where Jackie Arnold's expert guidance comes in. *Get That Job With NLP* draws on a wide range of NLP tools and Clean Language processes to make sure you are fully prepared. There are other books that give advice on this topic, but few ensure you prepare your most important asset – your mind – so thoroughly.

This book doesn't guarantee you will get the job you want, and it doesn't pretend there is a secret formula. Instead Jackie provides practical things that you can *do*. And while the focus is on employment, it is easy to see how many of the tools can be applied elsewhere: to presentations and public speaking; to sports or artistic performances; to tough conversations and negotiations; and many more.

Get That Job With NLP will give you the chance to prepare yourself to your highest ability and to perform at your best. It is not about fooling an employer into thinking you are something you are not. It is about presenting a true picture of you and all your qualities, skills and resources – not only as you are now, but also your potential to learn, grow and continually improve.

Then you can hold your head up high, knowing that you did all you could do to show yourself in the very best light.

James Lawley and Penny Tompkins

London, November 2012

Introduction

This book will aim to answer some of the questions you may have about how to find a job that you enjoy. It will address those feelings of demotivation and frustration you might have when faced with so many decisions. It will support you so that you feel more in control of the situation and can start out positively on your job search.

In my role as a coach and trainer I support people from all walks of life to present themselves well at interview. Often, even when you are well qualified and have experience, it is at the interview stage where the nerves kick in. Perhaps you have been out of work for a while or this is your first interview – whatever the case you will find useful interview tips and strategies here.

Get That Job with NLP focuses on enhancing interview skills and personal image using NLP and positive behavioural techniques. It will help you to plan, prepare and practise for your job interview using NLP and 'Clean Language' questions. You will also learn how to present yourself effectively on the day and gain coping strategies for both during the interview and when the interviews are over.

Approach

The book is in three parts: before the interview, during the interview and after the interview. You will discover case studies, tools and techniques you can learn from and use straight away. (Please note: all names in case studies have been changed.)

The book focuses on coping with rejection, building your confidence and enhancing your interview strategy in a variety of situations. It will give you a starting point to change an interview from a normal Q and A to a genuine discussion between adults. It will also help you to plan and think about a desired outcome and will hone your communication techniques to give you a distinct advantage at interview.

THE AIM OF THIS BOOK

This book aims to help you manage situations by changing how you think (cognitive) and act (behavioural) and how that can change your habits and unhelpful behaviours. It focuses on the positive aspects of situations and problems. The emphasis in this book is on assignments and exercises that will demonstrate your dedication to achieving your goal of finding a job. If you are willing to take time to complete these exercises you will gain the most benefit.

An introduction to NLP

Neuro-linguistic programming (NLP) was the result of a collaboration that began in 1970 at the University of California between Richard Bandler, a maths student, and John Grinder, a professor of linguistics. They identified and developed specific models of excellence.

NLP is essentially the study of how humans think, feel and behave to achieve the best results they can. It is done by modelling and replicating useful and forward-thinking strategies and behaviours.

▶ N = Neuro – how you use your senses to experience what is going on around you, including your physiology, your feelings, your actions and your patterns of speech.

▶ L = Linguistic – the use of specific language to communicate with self and others.

▶ P = Programming – the use of the brain to plan and achieve results and the impact you have on yourself and on others.

NLP PRESUPPOSITIONS

▶ Mind and body are parts of the same system, each affecting the other.

▶ The map is not the territory and the menu is not the meal: we all have different maps, menus and views of the world.

▶ Things often happen as we think or believe they will. Henry Ford (inventor of Ford motor cars) said: 'If you think you can do it, or you think you can't do it, you are probably right!'

▶ Modelling excellent behaviour leads to excellence. If one person can do something, others can learn to do it.

▶ There is no such thing as failure, only feedback (and renewed opportunity for success).

▶ The person with the greatest number of choices and most flexibility in a situation is likely to get the best result.

▶ The meaning of your communication is the response you get.

▶ Every behaviour is appropriate in some context. Most behaviours have a positive intention.

▶ The resources we need are within us. To some extent, we create our own experience.

▶ Communication is non-verbal as well as verbal, and non-conscious as well as conscious.

(Revell and Norman, 1997 and Elston and Spohrer, 2009)

Using Clean Language to help you find a job

What is Clean Language and symbolic modelling and how can it help me to find a job?

In this book you will have the opportunity to use a variety of techniques that may help you to explore different ways and approaches to finding a job. When counselling psychologist David Grove developed a technique called 'Clean Language' he had spent time watching and listening to the way people communicated. He realized that many who were in a supporting role were subtly re-wording what people were saying when communicating one to one. As a result he considered what kind of questions would contain fewer assumptions, yet still direct attention to areas of people's experience that seemed to need more thought or consideration. These are the 'clean' questions I often use with my clients. Throughout this book I encourage you to use them yourself as they can be very helpful in your quest to find a job. The questions provide a kind of feedback loop so that your thinking becomes clearer and new knowledge emerges.

Clean Language was originally used in therapy, but is now used in many different situations to enable people to problem solve and feel better about themselves and their future. It is a method that attends to your own specific language and poses a specific set of questions to elicit metaphors. These metaphors or symbols can be really useful in providing an anchor and stabilizing your thoughts both before and during the interview.

When using Clean Language, you use specific questions asked in a particular way. Some of these questions may seem odd and clunky to you. They certainly did when I first started using them. Please bear with me and give them a try even if you feel they seem different. The questions are designed to delve deeper into the underlying reasons for your job search, and to elicit metaphors that will help to anchor your thoughts. It is often useful to develop a strong inspiring image in your mind to 'hold on to' as you prepare and practise for interview.

The case studies throughout this book reproduce the Clean Language used in the original sessions. This involves repeating key phrases back to you (the client) so that you stay in your own thoughts. When this happens it is as if you have a continuous stream of consciousness. This is not interrupted by the coach (as they use your words) but allows you to continue to create your own view of the situation, cleanly. This technique helps to develop metaphors which in turn help you to understand and explain abstract concepts. This technique may seem a little unusual but is now used widely in interviews, for appraisals and business meetings, etc.

Clean Language is effective in that, when a variety of words are reflected back to the speaker in the order they have mentioned them, they retain a stream of consciousness. They are in their own space and hearing the familiar words they have just used helps them to understand their own thought process. They are clearer and feel valued and heard by the listener.

When *interviewers* use these techniques it can be very effective as they minimize their own assumptions, perceptions and language interference. As an *interviewee* it is useful for you to understand these techniques and apply them not only at interview but also in your workplace. The skills in this book are also useful for general communication and will enable you to enhance your relationships both at work and at home.

Two key NLP principles are:

1 You have control over your own thoughts and behaviours, not over those of others.

2 Keep doing the same and that's what you'll get – the same.

Visual, auditory and kinaesthetic representations

At this point you may be interested to know more about the meaning of VAK that I will be referring to throughout this book.

▶ **Visual:** You may be asked to describe the way you 'see' your job and to visualize various aspects of your role.

▶ **Auditory:** You may be requested to describe the sounds you hear when you are working or preparing for interview.

▶ **Kinaesthetic:** Sometimes you may need to describe the physical (tactile) feel of the working environment, your own feelings about it and be asked to list or place these so they can be seen and referred to.

As the NLP approach often involves the use of story-telling and metaphor, I will be using case studies and actual coaching sessions to illustrate some of the NLP and Clean Language techniques.

Ten questions you may be asking

1 *What is NLP?* Neuro-linguistic programming is the study of how humans think, feel and behave to achieve the best results they can.

2 *Who started it?* Richard Bandler, a maths student, and John Grinder, a professor of linguistics.

3 *How does it work?* It is done by modelling and replicating useful and forward-thinking strategies and behaviours used by successful people.

4 *How is it helpful for interviews?* It is based on proven successful communication techniques and behaviours, both verbal and non-verbal.

5 *How is it different from other methods?* It models excellence, and is positive and forward focused.

6 *How do I apply it?* By practising and applying the techniques, modelling effective behaviours and visualizing yourself succeeding.

7 *What is the first strategy I can adopt?* Have a specific desired outcome.

8 *What is rapport?* Building a relationship on trust and mutual understanding.

9 *How can I best create rapport?* By accepting and attempting to understand another's opinion and view of the world.

10 *What techniques and skills apply specifically to job applications?* Excellent communication skills, creating rapport,

greater awareness of self and others, setting and achieving goals, creating a positive mindset, visualization, building positive relationships.

It is therefore my intention to:

► Provide a 'multi-sensory' book with meaningful tasks, in which all readers are able to access their particular preferred representational systems (VAK) and where you can feel engaged and motivated in your job search.

► Create conditions in which you the reader feel comfortable and confident enough to express yourself, and use your personal experiences and feelings beyond those techniques you may have used before.

Part One

Before the Interview

Building Your Desired Outcome

In this chapter you will discover:

- *How to clarify the kind of role you are looking for*
- *How to build on your own strengths and skills*
- *Exercises to boost your confidence*
- *Strategies to succeed at interview*

If you are reading this you are obviously thinking about getting a job. Let's start with what kind of job you are aiming for. If you do not quite know what job you want, this exercise will stimulate those creative juices! It's a great exercise for anyone looking for or considering a new direction or first job.

Note: There will be exercises throughout this book that might challenge you, and there will be questions that may appear strange or a little awkward. Keep trying and you will find that they become easier as you go along. These are not random questions and the skills have been used effectively for years – persevere. If you want to find a job, then some effort and new skills will be needed to get you there!

Try it now: Future pacing

Take some time to sit in a comfortable chair and relax. Now begin to imagine yourself sitting in a rocking chair as an old pensioner without much to do. Looking back over your shoulder at your working life, what thoughts and memories would you like to have? As the old pensioner, imagine what jobs you had when you were younger. Think back to what you are proud of and what specific memories you can tell young relations about your life. Stay in this relaxed state as an old person and let your mind wander to the areas of your job that inspired you. Really imagine yourself working and being in that job you had and the stories you can tell as a result. If you are just starting out on the job path, imagine what jobs you would have in your ideal world.

Future pacing is an NLP technique to prepare you for action!

Still in the same position as the old pensioner, sitting in your chair looking back over your life, imagine how you would feel if you hadn't achieved that really good job – the pain of not having worked or found a job you enjoyed. If you are out of work now, notice the pain you feel and how uncomfortable that is. Are you ready for the work you need to put in to achieve your goal, and to bring about the change in your life?

Now imagine you had achieved your goal and had worked in a job you really enjoyed. How do you feel? What pleasure do you get from working and feeling you are contributing, using your skills or making a difference?

At this juncture it is important to consider your own mindset and beliefs. Some may be holding you back and preventing you from moving towards your goal.

One person might be saying to themselves:

▶ Other people should recognize my efforts and achievement.

▶ They must be aware of how hard I am working and the hours I put in.

▶ I am constantly frustrated by the methods used and have no power to change things.

Another person may be thinking:

▶ I am really happy with what I have achieved.

▶ I am working hard and getting good results – that's satisfying.

▶ I am frustrated by the methods used so I need to find a way to change things.

Neither view is right or wrong; however, everyone has filters and ways of viewing things. These patterns often stem from upbringing and education and are so habitual that they often go unnoticed. Being aware of your thought patterns can increase awareness and lead to more helpful and positive thinking.

Dwelling on what others should, must, or have to do can be unhelpful. One of the underlying principles of NLP is that you only have control over your own thoughts and behaviours, not over those of others.

Also, in preparation for your job search, you need to be challenging your own thoughts and feelings. Here are some ways of doing that so that you can get clarity and better understanding of what you really want.

You will find that your reactions to the exercises and statements in this book are beginning to form. Notice your own language and note down some of the phrases you use as you read through the chapters. This will aid your understanding and allow you to be aware of your own views of the world.

Generalizations

Here are some generalizations that you may notice yourself and others using on a daily basis. Ask yourself the questions that follow the statements and you will gain greater clarity and understanding of the issues:

▶ *I'm not sure.* Ask: About what exactly?

▶ *I don't know.* Ask: What exactly don't you know?

▶ *Everything is getting worse.* Ask: What is getting worse?

▶ *I really failed at that.* Ask: What specifically went wrong?

▶ *They really make me feel frustrated.* Ask: In what way do you feel frustrated?

Once you begin to notice generalizations such as 'always, never, everything, no one' you can ask yourself questions like those above. Finally, ask yourself questions beginning with 'What needs to happen...?'

For example:

▶ *I really failed at that!*

▷ What specifically went wrong?

▷ What needs to happen so that you are more successful next time?

▶ *I never seem to find the time!*

▷ What, never? Was there ever an occasion when you **did** find the time?

▷ What needs to happen for you to put time aside for this?

Really challenging your statements in this way can get to the heart of any issues that may arise and help you to avoid generalizing. In NLP terms this is called using meta model questions and can be really useful in a variety of business situations.

Now try this question: why do you need or want a job? This may seem obvious but it is useful for you to be sure.

Core values

What do you really value in a job and in your life?

If you are not sure, the exercise below can help you explore your values. It is useful to know what is important to you and what you care about.

Values form the basis of how you approach your life. What you value and how much you value it affect your attitudes, beliefs, choices and behaviours. For example, if you value 'space and a feeling of freedom' in your life, perhaps a job working nine to five in an office will not suit you. If however you really love 'organization and fixed routine' then an office job will not feel so constrained. If you value 'creativity' then being in a job that does not allow you the scope to be inventive and to create something may be restrictive. In some cases you may be forced to accept any job just because you really need one. However, you will never be content or successful if you work where your values are compromised. It is helpful to know your values as then you can always look for subtle ways to change your circumstances – even if the job role is not an ideal match. If you are not aware of this you will always wonder why you feel unhappy and discontented, even if the job seems to be a good one.

you have ever admitted this to yourself. Some of these you will know innately. Others require some frank 'soul-searching'. Ask yourself 'Why is this value important enough to me to be a True Value?' Write down five specific reasons.

3   Ask: Who am I when I am this value? How do I act? What do I think about? What do I feel? What motivates me?

For example:

Sam really values 'design' and he enjoys drawing and creating new designs for websites so he wrote:

> When I am designing I am totally focused on what I do. I forget I am working and enjoy the feeling of something new emerging. I love experimenting with new ideas and allowing them to float to the surface. I feel totally absorbed and the time passes quickly.

Answer the five questions above for each of your values.

4   Ask: Who am I not when I am this value? How do I behave? How do I feel about myself? About others? About life?

For example Sam wrote:

> When I am designing I am not bored and the day does not drag by. I am nice to be around. I feel contented and I am not frustrated or sharp with my colleagues, family or friends. In this job I am not feeling I don't want to go to work; instead I am motivated and getting up in the morning is not a chore.

Write down five specific responses for each value on a piece of paper. This enables you to be clear about what is really important to you

ADVENTURE	TO CATALYSE
Risk	Impact
The Unknown	Move forward
Thrill	Touch
Danger	Turn on
Speculation	Unstick others
Dare	Coach
Gamble	Spark
Endeavour	Encourage
Quest	Influence
Experiment	Stimulate
Exhilaration	Energize
Venture	Alter

TO DISCOVER

Learn

Detect

Perceive

Locate

Realize

Uncover

Discern

Distinguish

Observe

BEAUTY

Grace

Refinement

Elegance

Attractiveness

Loveliness

Radiance

Magnificence

Gloriousness

Taste

TO CREATE

Design

Invent

Synthesize

Imagination

Ingenuity

Originality

Conceive

Plan

Build

Perfect

Assemble

Inspire

TO CONTRIBUTE

Serve

Improve

Augment

Assist

Endow

Strengthen

Facilitate

Minister to

Grant

Provide

Foster

Assist

TO FEEL

Emote

To experience

Sense

To glow

To feel good

Be with

Energy flow

In touch with

Sensations

PLEASURE

Have fun

Be hedonistic

Sex

Sensual

Bliss

Be amused

Be entertained

Play games

Sports

TO LEAD

Guide

Inspire

Influence

Cause

Arouse

Enrol

Reign

Govern

Rule

Persuade

Encourage

Model

TO RELATE

Be connected

Part of community

Family

To unite

To nurture

Be linked

Be bonded

Be integrated

Be with

BE SENSITIVE

Tenderness

Touch

Perceive

Be present

Empathize

Support

Show compassion

Respond

See

TO TEACH

Educate

Instruct

Enlighten

Inform

Prepare

Edify

Prime

Uplift

Explain

MASTERY

Expert

Dominate field

Adept

Superiority

Primacy

Greatest

Best

Outdo

Set standards

Excellence

TO WIN

Prevail

Accomplish

Attain

Score

Acquire

Win over

Triumph

Predominate

Attract

BE SPIRITUAL

Be aware

Be accepting

Be awake

Relate with God

Devoting

Holy

Honouring

Be passionate

Religious

List kindly shared by Thomas Leonard, founder of Coach U

Try it now: What appeals?

This is a great exercise to do with a friend or colleague if that's possible.

Get hold of some national and local newspapers and circle in a bright colour those jobs you are attracted to. You are *not* concerned with what skills or knowledge they require at this stage. Just have fun! Circle a number of jobs that are *interesting*, no matter if you are qualified or not – play with this process and enjoy the experience. Forget the skills or the salary, just choose those that appeal to your values or sound interesting. Start noticing what you are drawn to and whether any patterns begin to form. Ask:

✳ What is common among all/some of the jobs you have circled?

✳ What else do you notice about them?

✳ What kind of jobs have you selected? Make a list for clarity.

✳ Use a coloured pen to circle any key words that you notice.

✳ What skills and knowledge are needed?

✳ If you feel this job is out of your reach, what might be a job in the same field that you could do?

✳ If you don't have the skills currently, are there ways you can train for them?

✳ Does your local enterprise agency run courses or free workshops?

✳ What roles have you had in the past that might be connected or similar?

✳ If you have identified some similarities, make a list of them.

✳ What do you know now that might help you move forward?

✳ Make a list of jobs that might be possible based on your findings.

✳ Expand your thoughts to include those that may be just out of reach – this may just be fear of the unknown or fear of failure.

✳ Really imagine what might be possible if you allow your thoughts to expand and test the water.

Reasons for your search

Are you frustrated with the job market and really want to take a different approach? Are you a mother or father returning to work? Perhaps you have been made redundant and are feeling your age may be an issue? Perhaps this is your first job and you are finding the job market a real challenge? Whatever position you are in, the techniques in this book will support you.

Your transferable skills

What skills have you picked up from your own experiences? There are plenty of skills and knowledge you already have and can offer. What are your hobbies? What duties have you held in clubs, at meetings or during casual jobs you may have held? Dig out all your knowledge and skills as many of them will be transferable. I strongly advise you to write down, create a diagram or draw a picture to represent your skills, knowledge and experience (see 'Try it now', below).

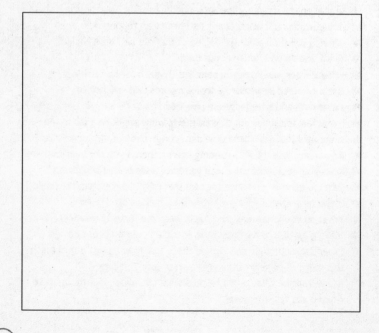

Case study

At a recent training session on interview skills I asked a participant what skills and experience he had for the role he was after. He replied that he had no skills that he thought were relevant. After asking him what he had done for the past couple of years he realized he had many transferable skills he had not taken into consideration.

✳ He had helped to run the local scouts club where his two young sons were members.
✳ He had given his mother help with her accounts.
✳ He had taken a local job delivering magazines.

After further discussion and questioning he discovered examples of several skills and qualities that he could take into account. Here are only some of those he came up with:

✳ The scouts club: Responsible and reliable, good organizational skills, friendly manner, approachable, good communication skills.
✳ Accounts: Good with figures and managing money, attention to detail, calm under pressure, good time management.
✳ Local job: Responsible, friendly manner, flexible worker, able to complete and finish a task successfully.

Remember this

Even if you have never worked before you may have helped a sibling or your family with housework or done a paper round. This means you are responsible, helpful and keen to learn. If you have been made redundant then think of all the transferable skills and knowledge you may have taken from your past roles. Have you held meetings, been part of negotiations or led a team? If you are a returning parent, then all you have learnt about raising your child will mean you have added to your skills.

Try it now: Your skills

Make a list of your skills or draw a picture or flow chart to clearly show your abilities and knowledge. Put the list in a place where you can see it on a daily basis.

Make it colourful and try using pictures. This is a powerful technique used by competitive athletes as it encourages the unconscious mind to focus on your strengths. If you find it hard to think of your skills and experience, ask someone to help you. Generally people are better at thinking about what others do well than themselves!

When answering the questions 'What job do I want?', 'What else do I want?' and 'What kind of role/position do I want?', keep working on your answer until you have it in 100% positive terms. Keep adding more details. Think about when and where you want to work, about who might be involved, and about what it will mean to you when you achieve it. Again this is exactly what athletes do when they want to achieve greater speeds or play even better. They focus on exactly what they want, where they will be and who will be with them. Put in as much detail as possible so that you can hear, feel, smell and visualize yourself in your new job. You may feel that this task is a little daunting, as success can sometimes be almost as fearful as having no job at all. However, I strongly suggest you give it a go. Try to make it light and fun. Doing these simple exercises will help to change your frame of mind towards a positive outcome.

Using visualization

Visualization is a very powerful NLP technique, which involves picturing what any new situation could look like. During visualization, the images you imagine stimulate your brain; effectively you are training your unconscious mind to prepare for an event or situation in advance. This enables you to feel more familiar with whatever comes up on the day. Really seeing that event clearly in your mind's eye, in colour and with anyone else involved will really help with any nerves or anxious thoughts.

Key idea

Step outside your own persona and just observe **another person** in your ideal job. What are they doing, seeing and hearing? What are they thinking and how are they feeling? What positive skills and behaviours are they displaying? Doing this enables you to pursue your ideal role and to visualize yourself in this role from the point of view of an observer. Often this can unlock the areas where you are feeling disheartened.

Case study

Jo* had been out of a job for three years. She lived in London with her husband but they had recently moved from Canada where she had also struggled to find work. In the end she worked part time as an external consultant but was not at all motivated. In London she had applied for seven different jobs without success. She sometimes made it to the interview stage but no further.

One very prominent barrier was her anger and frustration at not being accepted. The constant rejection had undermined her confidence and she was very vulnerable. She felt her skills were inadequate and she was never going to be successful.

I began by asking her what her strengths were and what skills and knowledge she had brought to her previous job, what had worked for her in the past and the projects she had developed for her previous employer. Slowly we built up a picture of her knowledge and past skills so she began to feel that she really did have something to offer. Next we focused on her recent interviews, what had gone well and where she felt she might have fallen short of what was required.

(Notice I am using the word feel/felt quite often as Jo's preferred representational system was definitely kinaesthetic. This means she spoke a lot about how things felt for her, for example she was 'frustrated and angry' and 'feeling vulnerable'.)

She had researched the jobs well and knew a lot about the companies. Her skills and knowledge matched the role and her CV was excellent. So when she got an interview she was delighted, only to fall at the final hurdle. I suggested we set up a live interview, so that I, in the role of interviewer, could see, feel and hear what was happening. This interview was videoed and I even asked her to dress as she would for a real interview.

It was very revealing. As she had been out of a job for a while she noticed she had acted very defensively. Her body language 'showed' us that she expected to fail and she became quite forceful at times. She made little or no attempt to create rapport and we were left feeling she would not succeed at interview in this frame of mind. When she saw the recording she was really surprised at how she came across. She couldn't believe her attitude and it was quite difficult for her to watch.

We then worked out a strategy using visualization and positive behavioural techniques. She began to 'see' and 'feel' herself in the interview as someone capable and with a positive attitude. She worked on creating rapport by using eye contact and a curious voice tone. We used affirmations (positive statements in the present) to build her confidence and gradually she began to change. Whenever she fell back into 'what if I fail?' mode she found a phrase to replace it: 'this time is different, this time I am giving myself a better chance'.

She identified the kind of job she wanted using sensory language. She wrote down all the criteria and then searched for her ideal position. She got an interview for two jobs and after spending time and visualizing herself as feeling confident and positive she was offered the job she now holds. It took three months for her to change her limiting assumptions and attitude but in the end she got the job she wanted.

*NB: All names in case studies have been changed.

VISUAL, AUDITORY AND KINAESTHETIC (VAK) PREFERENCES

We all have our preferred way of interpreting the world around us. Some of us are visually orientated (painters, sculptors, graphic designers, etc), some auditory (singers, broadcasters, language teachers, etc), while some prefer the active kinaesthetic expression and often choose caring professions. These are preferences, and most of us will use a combination of styles.

Try it now: Visual, auditory or kinaesthetic?

Now begin to think about what you want in terms of what you can see, touch, feel, taste, and smell. How will you know you have achieved your ideal job? What will you be doing, seeing, hearing, feeling in this role? This will encourage your subconscious mind to stimulate your motivation and creativity. Notice which representational system you prefer. Do you find it easy to 'see' or visualize things, or do you generally hear or feel them? One way to discover this is to ask how you pick up information.

Auditory: Do you like to listen to radio programmes, speeches or presentations? Do you find it easy to learn languages and pick up words from songs? Do you listen to people speaking and learn from them by taking notes or repeating/reading things back to yourself later?

Do you use language such as: 'I heard that...', 'I picked that up from...', 'I didn't quite catch what you said', 'I hear that the event was really good', 'It sounds like you had a good time'.

Kinaesthetic: Do you feel/sense what is happening around you and tend to buy products or services with emotion rather than reason? When you feel an emotion does it stay with you or can you shake it off quickly? Are some of your possessions tactile (made of fur or soft materials that you enjoy the feel of)?

Do you use language such as: 'I feel that...', 'I just had a gut feeling that...', 'I think she felt it was a poor judgement', 'I feel really strongly about that', 'What do you feel about that?', 'It really sent a shiver down my spine', 'I have a funny sensation/premonition that x might happen'.

Visual: Do you enjoy watching and looking at things in order to make sense of them? Do you draw or doodle when speaking on the phone? Do you have a wall chart even if you use a computer?

Do you enhance your surroundings with colour and use language such as: 'Yes I see', 'Yes, I've noticed that', 'I'll take a look at that and get back to you', 'In my view...', ' As I see it...', 'it looks/appears to me like...'.

We all use all of these expressions from time to time, as no one is exclusively V, A or K. However, we usually have a preference and it is interesting to notice your own. It is also useful to notice other people's preference as then we can understand them better. A secondary school teacher I know who works with NLP always ensures he is using all of the senses with his pupils. In this way he engages the whole class and does not allow his own preferences to dominate.

One of my clients, a university student, knows that she learns much better when she hears something rather than reads it. When she listens to lectures she can pick up the meaning quickly and can also understand how the techniques might be applied in reality. However, when she reads from manuals she finds it hard to concentrate and retain the facts. This is useful for her to know, as then she can record important passages and listen to them to aid her studies. She has found this very effective.

Most people have visual tendencies to a greater or lesser degree. We are bombarded with visual stimuli wherever we go and have learned to notice posters, magazine pictures, TV promotions and advertisements.

Visualization is such a powerful tool that I encourage you to practise and increase your skills in this area. It simulates the subconscious which inspires you and gives you creative ideas. It is also linked to the creation of metaphors and you will be asked to create your own as you read through the book.

For example: You might visualize a job working as a production assistant in a film company and then, quite unexpectedly, you begin to see adverts for this kind of job quite often. The part of the brain we call Reticulated Activating System (RAS) has been activated, causing you to notice jobs you may not have seen before. Visualization causes you to notice something as soon as you place your focus on it. If you focus on yellow cars you will begin to see them on a regular basis – if you think about red cars you will see them everywhere too. Where we put our focus is where the brain 'tunes in' and enables us to notice where before we may not have.

Visualizing your new job can help to create motivation, new ideas, and creativity because your subconscious starts to believe it can be possible. Humans need motivation and a reason to get up in the morning. Positive emotions and pictures you create in your mind are the stimulation you need to enable you to take action on finding your next job. You start to believe that this job can be yours and so you are motivated to take action. Taking action is the key to keeping you on a positive path towards your job. Even one small action a day can really make a difference to how you feel and think about your future.

Actually, you are not visualizing for the first time. You have used these techniques most of your life – you were just not so conscious of it. Think for a moment about how you thought about your first girl or boy friend. Did you imagine how they might look and what they might wear for your first date? What about your first car? Did you think about or see one in your mind's eye before you actually started looking? Most people do this kind of visualizing without being conscious of it. It is only when you really begin to focus your attention on it that the subconscious begins to take it seriously.

Try it now: Positive visualizations

Start to make positive visualizations about the job you would like.

Visualize working in this job now in the present and how you feel and think about it.

Evoke all the positive emotions and senses to inform your subconscious that this is what you really want. Take your time over this as you need to banish all those voices and negative thoughts that have been around before. Replace them with new positive visualizations just before you go to bed and again in the morning.

Use pictures connected to your job that excite you and help you to 'see' yourself working in this new role. Place yourself in the picture and really begin to form an idea of what the environment looks like, who is with you and what you are doing.

If you keep doing this you will retrain the subconscious mind and help it to focus on the positive aspects of your job search. You will discover that after a few weeks you will begin to have more motivation and enthusiasm for this journey.

Also try using affirmations to re-enforce these images. Affirmations are positive statements in the present tense as if you have already achieved them. For example:

✳ I am working in a great job that I enjoy.
✳ I have people around me I like working with.
✳ I am skilled in the areas I need for this job.
✳ I feel motivated and willing to learn.

Continue these affirmations until you have written about ten. The best thing to do is to write them down and then read them just before you go to bed. While you are asleep your subconscious mind will work on them for you.

It may seem a little strange to write things that are not yet true. However, this is probably what you did when you were young. You might have thought about how or what you would be when you grew up and how learning a new skill might help you in the future. The only difference is that you are now doing this with deliberation and focus. You need to start to believe you will succeed. This is hard when you can't see how this can come about. However, this is what top achievers do, be they athletes, business leaders or successful pop stars.

Having faith in yourself will enable you to climb out of your lack of motivation or your 'this won't work' mode. As long as you are in that state you give yourself no chance at all. If you don't allow yourself to think about succeeding in your job search you will not attract the people, roles or workplace that you are looking for.

PREPARING TO VISUALIZE

When you start your visualization, look at your motivating pictures and read your affirmations before you begin. Then sit in a comfortable chair and breathe deeply from the diaphragm. Allow your mind to relax and drift into the picture of your in your new job role. Really begin to see yourself in this role with all that is going on around you. Use the senses and feel what it's like to be there and experience the sensations of challenge, learning, excitement and enthusiasm. Slowly say your affirmations and make each of them real and current.

When I was writing my first book on public speaking, I felt that I was not good enough and that no one would read what I had to say. I told myself that I was deluding myself and that I was not a writer. Of course I did not manage to write anything for quite a long time. However, I met someone who had written a book and who suggested I 'created' rather than tried to 'write' a book. This appealed to me and I began to visualize what my book might look like and how I could create a book that people would read. I began to think about myself as a creative writer and I wrote some affirmations to inspire me. Slowly my positive thoughts began to overcome my initial doubts and one day I sat down and began to write.

As you do your visualizations your motivation will grow and you will slowly find yourself feeling more positive. Notice how your body feels different and allow the different sensations to flow through you. If the visualization works better outside your home, take a walk and begin to imagine and start looking into a different more interesting future.

I suggest setting aside ten minutes a day for visualization and another ten minutes for affirmations as this will really help to develop a positive mindset. The best time is just before you go to bed as this allows your subconscious mind to work on the positive visualization. Read the affirmations again when you get up in the morning.

Give it a go!

Using Clean Language and developing metaphors

One way of starting the process of developing a metaphor for yourself is to ask: 'When I am working at my best, I'm like... [what]?' Once you have found an image or a colourful thought you then ask: 'And is there anything else about... [your image or thought]?' to develop it further. We use metaphors all the time in our daily lives without even thinking about it. They enable us to show clearly what we mean and are often a quick way to get our message across. Metaphors are a way of explaining something clearly in terms of something else. If you enjoy watching sport then here are some examples you might recognize:

- The game is just **getting under way.**

- They're playing a **waiting game.**

- She's **in the zone.**

- They're making **heavy weather of it.**

- He's taking **a gamble.**

In daily life, we might use similar metaphors such as:

- I'm **running behind** today.

- I'm feeling **a bit down.**

- She's **taking that a bit hard.**

- He's **onto a winner.**

- They've had **a stroke of luck.**

The questions that follow in 'Try it now' will encourage you to focus your attention on the metaphorical as this can be a powerful stimulus.

Try it now: Ask questions

Answer this question: For you to be working at your best **you** will be **like** ... what?

To help you with this question I will share with you what a client, Clare, answered:

> For me to be working at my best I will be **like** an expert dancer. I will enjoy the music and hear the different sounds and focus on my environment. I will listen to the beat of the music and feel part of it. I will sway with the rhythm and other people will join me in the dance.

When asking these questions of yourself think about what **you** would be like. For example, you might say: 'I'd be like when I'm playing tennis, very focused on my position on the court, not always getting it right, yet really enjoying the game and feeling relaxed.'

Or: 'I'd be like an inventor always looking for a different challenge and experimenting with ideas and solutions.'

Think about what you would **be like** in your chosen role or profession and develop a strong metaphorical image for your new job.

Then follow this up with (using your own words): 'An expert dancer, and **is there anything else about** that expert dancer when you are working at your best?'

So your question to yourself will be: '[Your example] **and is there anything else about** [your example].

Then ask yourself another question: 'For this work to be just the way you want it to be, **it** would be **like** ... what?'

Clare answered:

> It would be challenging. I would need to be using my brain and my creativity so I guess for me it would be like driving my new car. I want to rise to the challenge, I want to learn. Even when it seems that I need to do several things at once I can practise until it becomes second nature. Sometimes it will push me into the fast lane and other times it will be parked at the roadside so I can think things through.

I followed this question with: 'And like driving a new car ... and when like driving a new car, what kind of car is that, when your work is the way you want it?'

She replied: 'It's a blue VW Beetle, it's got enough power to hold its own on the motorways yet is small enough to manage safely. I would feel comfortable in the driving seat and know that it will perform well in all weathers.'

Clare had found a strong metaphor she could relate to. It would help her stay focused and motivate her every time she thought of it.

By developing these questions you are creating an outcome that is within your control. When you are working with a strong metaphor you will be able to keep it more easily in your mind. You become more confident and are clear about what it is you want and how you need to be.

We all know through our studies of NLP and neuroscience that the unconscious mind is considerably more powerful than the conscious mind. Surely if we can tap into that directly rather than going through our conscious mind with all of its filters, we are going to get better results.

Case study

Ruth (not her real name) is a very intelligent and competent lady in her thirties who is looking at a new career and considering her next steps. Her main issue is her lack of confidence, worrying too much about making mistakes and being too much of a perfectionist.

Her desired outcome was 'to have a strategy to gain confidence, put the past aside and move forward'.

During the second coaching session she mentioned that the voice in her head was like a small kitten so, as I had attended a workshop on the use of 'Clean Language' and the development of metaphors, I decided to use this technique to help her move forward.

I started the session by repeating her words and then asking the first 'clean' question:

(C: Coach, R: Ruth)

C: And when the unwelcome voice in your head is like a small kitten, what kind of kitten is that?

R: A black kitten with long hair.

C: And is there anything else about that kitten?

R: It is a bubbly, playful kitten and wants to do the right thing.

(We explored what 'the right thing' was and this gave Ruth new insights into the perfectionist mindset that was blocking her. We then returned to the metaphor of 'a small voice like a kitten'.)

C: And where could the kitten come from?

(It transpired that the voice in her head like a small kitten only arrived when Ruth had left home and no longer worked for her father.)

C: And is there anything else about the kitten?

R: Yes, it keeps waking me up at night and won't leave me alone at weekends.

C: What happened just before the kitten?

R: I knew who I worked for and trusted my manager completely.

C: And is there anything else about trust like that?

(It transpired that in Ruth's first job after leaving the company where she trusted the manager she had been bullied. The voice of the small kitten was her defence mechanism to protect herself. She now had difficulty trusting people and wanted a strategy so that she could control the voice inside her head [the kitten] and focus on the way forward.)

C: And control the voice, and trusting people and playful and wants to do the right thing and strategy, and is there anything else about that strategy?

R: I want to ensure that the kitten is locked in the kitchen so it can't disturb my sleep and I can have control over it when it wakes up. That way it only serves as a reminder and doesn't prevent me from moving forward with my goal.

C: And Ruth, what difference does knowing all this make to you?

R: I know that the kitten voice can be controlled and that I can shut it out when I want to. That gives me more confidence to take the next steps.

Case study contributed by Neil Williams, NLP Master Practitioner

Often the use of metaphor can unlock thoughts that have stayed in place for a while and refuse to budge. They are old habits and voices that get in the way and unless we address them will continue to block the path to the desired outcome.

Using metaphor and tapping into her unconscious mind, Ruth was able to take control of her life. She regained the confidence in her own ability to change things and could focus on her job search.

Staying in control

Are you in control or out of control?

When you are feeling vulnerable one of the best ways to feel stronger is to take control of those areas that you can have some influence on. Often when things are tough there is a tendency to think that everything is against you; that there is nothing you can do and nothing you can control. With a little space and time to think you may change that opinion. There are always aspects of a situation you are in control of and it helps to consider what they are.

Key idea

Think about what areas of the job interview you are in control of. These could be: the way you research; your knowledge of the company; the clarity around your role; how you need to behave in this job; your attitude towards it; what time you arrive; your appearance and so on.

You are in control of so much. Of course the decision to employ you lies with the company – but if you stay focused and don't allow rejection or dejection to deter you, you will stand a much better chance at interview.

The next question to ask yourself is: what could stop you from getting the job you want?

Sometimes being stuck has its advantages. You don't have to get up in the morning. No need to wear smart clothes or speak to anybody. I am sure this is not you as otherwise you wouldn't be reading this. However, ask yourself what you need to find a good job. What is it that will make a difference to you? What are your values and needs, what would or could you do without? If you have fears around the interview, ask yourself what is fact and what is fiction. What are you imagining might happen and what is really true?

Try it now: Fact and fiction

Look at the list below. Write down what is actually the situation (fact) and what you imagine it might be (fiction). I often use this technique when coaching my clients – to access a free coaching session go to www.coach4executives.com. If you prefer to do this alone, then try this now.

Some responses may be obvious, but sometimes they can trigger thoughts and emotions that allow you insights into your subconscious mind.

Statement	This is fact	This is fiction
If this job/interview were available **now**, would you take it?		
If you were offered an interview **now**, would you go?		
How prepared would you be and what is in your control and what is not?		
How could you be better prepared?		
What resources do you need to succeed?		
Do you have any support?		
If not, where can you access the support you need?		
Do you have a family member or a colleague to help you along the way?		
Do you need training?		
Where would be the best place to find this?		
How long is it since you were in a job?		
Can you afford to wait and for how long?		

Finally try this: In your mind's eye, put yourself into your ideal job. Really see, hear, feel, smell, touch what it would be like. What are you doing and saying? How are you behaving? Who is there? What can you see in front of you? Are you inside or outside: at a desk, in a shop, in a company or elsewhere?

The desired outcome

When you start out on the job search you need to come up with a well-formed desired outcome to get your conscious and subconscious minds working together. The desired outcome should also be motivating and have accountability so that you can achieve it. For your desired outcome to develop it needs focus and clarity.

As in the above exercise, start with this question:

▶ Consider your job in positive terms – what would it be like?

Give yourself time to consider all the possibilities.

Follow it up with 'Is there anything else I want?' and 'What kind of [your words] do I want?' until you have a very clear picture/ thought/idea that is both motivating and inspiring. You will know when this feels right for you. The job you want needs to cover: skills, knowledge, qualifications, environment, type of tasks, projects, location, travelling time, salary and conditions, as well as all the roles you would consider – the more specific you are the easier your search will become. Concentrate on the positive areas of the job, the tasks you are good at, the experience you have. No matter how small, no matter how trivial, every role you have had in the past will have something to offer you. Too many people tend to focus on what they don't want. NLP combats this, as the focus is on the positive and forward action. Ask: And when this job is just what I want and I am using my skills and knowledge is there anything else about a job like that?

Draw, list or make a diagram of what comes into your mind. Take some time to think and let your mind delve into the corners of your awareness.

Mental preparation is vital before you start looking for a job as this will greatly affect your interview performance. What are your current thoughts and feelings about getting a job? If you feel demotivated and you tend to think you are wasting your time, this can really affect your chances. It is, however, totally understandable, and feelings of apprehension and nervousness are part of this process. So channel these feelings and use them to understand how to change the negative beliefs you hold or that surround you. If for a moment you were to think in a positive way about finding a job – what difference would this make to your attitude? How would you be without those limiting assumptions? Take each step one at a time and see this as an investment in your future and a way to pull yourself into a more fulfilling life. It is hard when you are not in control of your future and have been knocked back. The good news is that you *can* change this and there are many things that you can do to improve your situation.

Case study

A reminder about the use of Clean Language in case studies: the client's words are often repeated back using key words. As these words come directly from the client the coach can keep it simple. The client will understand and stay in touch with their own mind as the coach is not contaminating their thought process. The coach is not introducing their own words or using intrusive questions. This is the power of Clean Language as no assumptions muddy the waters.

(C: Coach, A: Andy)

A: I'd like to find a job I enjoy.

C: And when you want to find a job you enjoy, what kind of enjoy is that?

A: It's an exciting feeling, maybe a little daunting but I think I'm up for the challenge!

C: And is there anything else about that job, when it's a job you enjoy?

A: Yes, it's a job where I feel accepted and where I am happy to get up in the morning most of the time.

C: And where is a job you enjoy?

A: Umm, it's fairly local if possible but I would be willing to travel if the job was as I described I guess.

C: And when that job is local, you're willing to travel, you feel accepted and happy to get up in the morning, you're excited and up for the challenge and it's a job you enjoy, is there anything else about a job like that?

A: Err... [thinks for a few minutes] I would like to be able to work with social media as I really enjoy the buzz that gives me. It would allow me to interact with people too and learn more about working in this field.

C: And learn more and interact with people and you'd enjoy the buzz it gives you. And when buzz what kind of buzz is that when you are working in social media?

A: It's as if I am now really part of a team and we are all working together. They accept me and I am enjoying the challenge of the day ahead.

C: And when you are part of a team and there's a buzz, that's a buzz like ... what?

A: I am getting the sense of bees round a hive all working together as one. We're achieving amazing things and I'm really contributing to the whole. It feels safe and yet challenging at the same time.

C: And when you have a job where you feel a buzz, it's challenging, you're part of a team and you want to get up in the morning ... then what happens?

A: Then I can feel more motivated and the days don't drag and my confidence grows.

C: And confidence grows and motivated and you want to get up in the morning and challenging and you feel a buzz and achieving amazing things and a job you enjoy and when all of that, then what happens?

A: Oh then I'll be earning money and perhaps start to look for a flat of my own to rent as I am really wanting to move out of my parent's house.

C: So are you ready to take the first steps to finding that job you enjoy?

A: Yes, let's go for it!

In the above case study, Andy is thinking about what might be possible. He is beginning to visualize what kind of job he would like and how that might look and feel. Some questions I asked were deliberately using Andy's language. For example: 'What are you thinking?' presupposes that you are *thinking* something, and limits your possible responses (Grove and Panzer, 1989), so I just asked Andy: 'Is there anything else about that job, when it's a job you enjoy? (using his words)

When you begin to ask yourself these questions, you will only use your own words and thoughts – this will help you to get clarity about what you want.

I wanted to be specific about where Andy was directing his attention, so I asked: 'What kind of enjoy is that?' or 'What kind of buzz is that?'

Since your experience of finding a job is happening now (even if you're recalling a memory) these questions are also asked in the present tense. As Clean Language is used extensively as an interviewing tool this book also shows you how to use it to facilitate your own thought process and guide you through your interview.

USING CLEAN QUESTIONS

Try beginning with these questions as a tool for finding a job. If you can, enlist the help of a colleague or a friend who is also looking for a job. Working with someone else on this can really be motivational.

Now ask yourself this first question:

▶ And what kind of job would I like?

If you are not sure, ask:

▶ And what kind of jobs do I seem to be interested in?

▶ What kind of hobbies or leisure activities do I enjoy?

This helps to identify what you want.

This question is followed up by asking a series of questions (Grove and Panzer, 1989). Now let's try some questions about individual words and phrases around your own job search (you can use another word in place of 'search').

For example:

▶ And is there anything else about [search]?

▶ And what kind of [search] is that?

▶ And where is that [search]?

▶ And what happens just before you [search]?

▶ And when you have [searched] for a while then what happens?

▶ And what needs to happen for you to continue your [search]?

Asking these questions helps you to slow down and enables you to think about what you really mean by 'search' or 'work' or 'job'.

Try it now: Ask questions

Let's assume that you are reading this book in order to find a job and be successful at interview.

Let's take the words 'find a job'.

The first logical clean question could be 'What kind of job is that?' but we are then assuming you already know what kind of job you want. (If you know what job you want now then answer that question and see what you come up with – write it down before you continue.)

To help you to get clarity on the kind of job you are looking for we will use the example of my client – Andy.

Andy said he wanted 'to find a job I enjoy' so I asked: 'And when you want to find a job you enjoy, what kind of enjoy is that?'

He replied, 'I am getting the sense of bees round a hive all working together as one. We're achieving amazing things and I'm really contributing to the whole. It feels safe and yet challenging at the same time.'

So, to learn more about the kind of job **you** want, try answering the following questions, taking time to think about your answers.

✻ When you want to find a job you enjoy, what kind of enjoy is that?
✻ And is there anything else about that job, when it's a job you enjoy?
✻ And where is a job you enjoy?

* And when all the things you have mentioned above come together to create a job you enjoy, that's like ... what? (encouraging a metaphor or visual image to emerge)
* And when you have a job you enjoy, then what happens?
* And what happens next?
* And are you now ready to take the first steps to finding that job you enjoy?

If your answer is not quite 'yes' then ask this question:
* What needs to happen for me to take that first step?

To develop your desired outcome further (finding a job you enjoy) try answering these questions:
* If you had a job you enjoy, **it** would be like ... what? (Remember times when you have been comfortable in a situation or role in the past.)
* If you had your ideal job **you** would need to be like ... what? (Think about what you would be feeling, seeing, thinking and behaving like.)

NEGATIVE BELIEFS

These might be beliefs you have held for a number of years and have become old habits. They are often in the form of stories such as:

> I am no good at interviews. Every time I go to an interview I always feel anxious and never seem to get my points across succinctly.

Or:

> I don't have the right skills and whenever I think about my skills I feel tense in my stomach. It generally takes me far longer than others to do things at first and then I end up rushing and making mistakes.

The key words in the first example are 'no good', 'every', 'always' and 'never'. In the second one: 'don't have', 'right', 'whenever', 'generally' and 'far longer'.

Notice that these words are generalizations. In order to get to the heart of the limiting belief you need to get the evidence. Check your responses with questions (What kind of? What happens just before X? What needs to happen for you to X?) to see if you really do have this feeling at 'every' interview, and are 'never' able to get a point across. Of course there will be times when you can find plenty of evidence to prove your beliefs. After all, this may have been an excuse to get you out of having to go for an interview or consider your skills. There is often some kind of payoff! All you need to do is encourage yourself to seek out the positive aspects of the situation. ('When have you managed to do X successfully in the past?' or 'What would you *like* to have happen?') Ideally, you will discover that there have been times when you have made a point successfully at interview or managed to complete tasks calmly and successfully.

Completing the following exercise you may discover new insights.

Try it now: Ask yourself

* What is my limiting belief?
* What evidence do I have to support this belief?
* How is this belief less than accurate or exaggerated?
* What is keeping this belief helping me to do?
* What caused me to cultivate this belief – where did this come from? So do these assumptions still apply?
* Has there ever been a time when this belief did not apply?
* Have I ever managed to make a useful point at interview?

Changing to an empowering belief

* What past experience can I draw on to support this new belief? (If no evidence is forthcoming, imagine how a new belief could be.)
* Who do I know who demonstrates this belief? (Think about people you know who appear confident and who you could model.)
* What will happen if I hold this new belief going forward?
* What can I do to maintain this belief?

At first you may not completely go along with this new belief. The old one has become a habit and it is like paddling down a river that is flowing fast and then having to change and paddle back up again against the current. I encourage you to keep trying it out. After you build up this new evidence, you will be able to build on it and it will become easier.

Focus points

The main points to remember from this chapter are:

- You need to develop a clear desired outcome and job role.
- Explore your own transferable skills, knowledge and qualities.
- Get into a positive and forward-looking mindset.
- Notice what is fact and what is fiction.
- Visualize your ideal position and what you will be thinking, seeing, hearing, smelling and touching (using all the senses to explore) when you are in that role.
- Use Clean Language to help move forward.

Next step

In the next chapter, we will look at taking these strategies forward a further step in the process. When you have identified the kind of role you are looking for, we will consider how you go about applying and marketing yourself to potential employers. We will discuss what specific communication skills you need and how to create rapport with your interviewer(s).

Job Applications

In this chapter you will discover:

- ▶ *The importance of your work experience and personal history*
- ▶ *The importance of researching the company you want to work for*
- ▶ *Communication techniques*
- ▶ *How to market yourself*

Work and personal history

Now is the time to think about your own job history and experience. Note down roughly what kind of companies you have been involved with up to now, the jobs you have held if any, and the roles you had at school and college. Even if you have not worked before you still have vital skills to focus on – everyone does. Cast your mind back to school: what were you good at? What did people come to you for? Did you win a prize for anything? What specific subjects were you good at? Have you done a Saturday job or helped your relatives out? Note all these answers down and keep writing till you have exhausted every skill you have and tasks you have done.

If you have worked before, what are your preferred roles and tasks? What are you good at? What motivates you? What do you value above all else in a job? What do you need to have/know/achieve to be really committed to the job?

List all the jobs/roles you have held and notice the patterns emerging. Then write your job history in date order with the most recent first. Briefly give the following information: date, name of company, your role, your responsibilities and reason for leaving.

For example:

> 2007–12, ABC Company, Marketing Manager, Marketing and promotion of products, corporate image and branding, product research.

(For yourself note down the specific skills and knowledge you gained – for use later.)

Then do the same for your personal history: date, name of role/task/hobby/activity, club or venue, skill/knowledge, awards/certificates/achievements.

For example:

> 2006, Team leader, Scouts, motivating others, team work, organization, time keeping, assertiveness, collaboration, best team leader award 2007.

This is time very well spent as it will inform the rest of your preparation and interview technique.

Research the company

A good place to start your research is the internet.

1 Make a list of all the areas where you match the job description and align your skills and knowledge to specific areas.

2 Notice the language of the job description as you read it and note down key words that are used.

3 These key words should be inserted into your CV and covering letter so that you are effectively matching their language. *(Note: Only use the words if they really apply to you and are genuinely part of your own experience and knowledge.)*

4 Think about and visualize examples you can give where your experience or knowledge could be useful in this role.

5 Try to match some of the language used in the job description with the skills and experience you have had.

Key idea: Matching the language of the company or interviewer

Interviewers will relate to you better when you match their language patterns. For example, if you are asked how you 'view' a situation use visual words in your response. If you are asked what you 'feel' about something then try to access your own feelings rather than responding with facts. If you match the employer's language in your CV and in your interview, you will instantly create rapport. The language you write will be what they are used to and create an instant relationship.

For example, if the advertisement or job description asks for 'experience in dealing with personnel issues and data protection' and you write you have had 'experience working with people and ensuring confidentiality', that's correct but you haven't used the language they are familiar with. This is only a small example of how language can be vitally important when preparing your CV, covering letter and your own interview questions.

✻ Always research as much as you can about the company before you go for an interview.

✻ Every company has a website, so look through and read their mission statement and underlying values.

* Find out what the company is involved in and read any articles or blogs you can find.
* Take a look at the 'about us' section to get a feel for who they are.
* Think about what you would like to ask them based on your research.
* Watch any videos or podcasts on the website to gain extra insights.
* Gather some knowledge of their products or services.
* Obtain and research the company's sales brochures and see if you can get hold of any company 'in-house' magazines or newsletters.
* Ask for a detailed job description.

Once you have done your research you are ready to move onto the next stage of preparation.

Communication techniques

Nearly every day you speak on the telephone or on your mobile. Admittedly, it's generally to one person at a time, but you have no script and no one to prompt you. It's automatic; you just speak with your own ideas and unique voice. Often you will pick up the phone and tell someone about an incident that has happened. You may chat about a recent holiday. Perhaps you need to arrange some business with a colleague. You don't give this a second thought despite it being a form of 'off the cuff' speaking as you will be doing at interview.

What about the impromptu speaking you do in a face-to-face situation? The visit you make to the bank to arrange an overdraft or set up an account. The complaint you make to your local authority about a public service. The time you stood up and asked a question at a meeting. Did you write the script before you went? No, of course not. You trust your own ability to speak whatever the situation.

It is very encouraging to recall the times when you have spoken to complete strangers without a script and without fear of getting it wrong. The skills you use on these occasions are the same as those you need at interview. It makes no difference if you have spoken one to one or to small groups at meetings or clubs. You already have all the tools you need to speak in front of that interview panel. With the help of this book you will begin to build on them and develop new skills and techniques. So don't panic – just prepare really well.

One comforting thought is that you are the only person who knows what you are going to ask. If you miss a couple of points, you can always add them later – no one will know. If someone invites you to come for an interview, take heart that others see you as interesting and competent. The key is to boost your self-esteem and confidence, then you will be able to handle the situation without fear. You will come to realize that you have the exact same value as those you will be speaking to.

In order to banish those butterflies you need to make the decision not to panic, but to prepare, plan and practise – the three Ps. Let's take the following case study as an example.

Case study

Matt had come to me to gain confidence before a really important interview. He belonged to the local Lions Club and often helped to raise funds for the community. He was also active in organizing events and days out for the local youth club in his area. One day he was invited for interview after months of sending off CVs and applying for jobs. He found himself feeling very anxious and afraid. Together we looked at his recent experience and how he had used his powers of persuasion to raise funds and to speak to the young people in his care. He understood that he had been both confident and convincing when asking for donations. He felt motivated when he realized that he had spoken to large groups of unruly teenagers and succeeded in holding their attention. He began to realize that this experience could help him and he developed ways to build on this. He decided not to panic – but to plan, prepare and practise well.

PREPARING AND WRITING YOUR CV

Now for your CV – do you have an existing one? Do you need one from scratch? You can search the internet for plenty of advice on writing a CV but here are a few tips to get you started.

▶ Keep your CV to a maximum of two pages.

▶ It should be typed neatly and have a positive tone.

- Start with noting your skills, knowledge and qualifications that are directly relevant to the job.

- Note down all the positive aspects of your career – you are marketing yourself here!

- Think about in what aspects of this job you can really shine and why.

- Let people know about your club memberships and outside interests and activities. This can be a real selling point to employers.

- In the professional profile area of your CV make sure you speak about your strengths and what makes you a good candidate.

- Visit people's professional profiles on LinkedIn – look out for words and phrases that you relate to and adapt them.

- As you write your CV, imagine you have already got an interview for your ideal job. Now put yourself in the position of the interviewer and check your CV for the qualities, experience, knowledge and skills you would be looking for. As an interviewer, what kind of person would you be looking for?

- Now go back to your CV and add anything you have missed or feel would match these requirements in terms of your own experience.

- Have you included your name, address, phone number, email, qualifications, and work history (even part-time or temporary work counts), as well as hobbies and leisure activities?

- Possible additions could be personal achievements, awards, and key strengths.

- Provide at least two references with contact details if requested.

- Stay positive and be gentle with yourself – nobody is perfect!

- Remember that your CV is your personal brochure – would you be interested in reading it?

- Keep your CV handy when you telephone for information on a position or have a telephone interview.

► Take your CV into the interview room, even if you have already sent it. This can act as a memory aid on the day.

COVERING LETTER AND WHAT TO INCLUDE

Your covering letter should be considered carefully as this could be your chance to gain an interview – or not! Put some time aside to consider:

► The wording of the advertisement or job description.

► How your skills and knowledge match their requirements.

Then start your letter with:

Dear [Ideally you will have a name for the addressee, if not Sir/ Madam],

Please find enclosed my CV in application of the post/position of [job title] *in* [name of paper or website] *advertised on* [date].

I am particularly suited to this position as I [find your own experience or skills to match the requirements and say how and when you demonstrated them]. *This involved* [x] *and I was able to* [x] *so that* [state a positive result].

I am able to [show your skills/knowledge in another area] *as I was* [x] *in a previous position or role.*

This position offers the opportunity to extend my skills and knowledge [give an example] *and I hope you will consider my application favourably.*

I am happy to supply references if you require them [or include them if they were requested with relevant details].

I look forward to hearing from you

Yours sincerely, [Yours faithfully if you wrote Sir/Madam]

Signature [Type your name under your signature.]

The letter above can be adapted for a speculative covering letter when you are not sure if a position is available. The first sentence should then be along the lines of:

I am writing to enquire whether you have a vacancy for [job role] *and I enclose my CV for your attention.*

EMAILS – CREATING A GOOD IMPRESSION

During your job search you may be corresponding by email.
The key NLP techniques of matching, mirroring and leading
will also apply here. If you have already received emails from
a company you are researching, take time to study them.
By matching the style of their emails you will create instant
rapport and this will give you a distinct advantage.

I work with several different people who all have different
styles of email correspondence. Some write long sentences
and are very 'chatty' in style, others write short sentences
with as few words as possible. Some will sign their name
with no salutation such as 'kind regards' or 'speak soon' or
'all the best' and to me this seems abrupt. To them it's just
being efficient and economical with words. No style is right
or wrong so it is useful to notice what people prefer. My
colleague who is economical with words finds it a waste of
time to read four sentences when two will do! So I avoid
sending him emails with long sentences and chatty phrases.

When you are corresponding with a variety of recruiters and
employers by email, notice the style they prefer. Do they have
a specific way of greeting you and signing off? How long are
their sentences? In general is the email long or short? How
much detail do they provide and what is the tone of the email?
Look for any language patterns and notice key words and
phrases. Then create rapport by using the same style as theirs.
Here's an example using some key words (starred *) and
similar tone and style.

▶ **Incoming email**

Chris,

Re: Application for Software Developer

> Thanks very much for sending in your application for the
> position advertised in IT Press last week. We have been
> inundated with applications and are currently drawing up
> a short list.

> We would be delighted to offer you the chance to attend
> an interview on Monday 21st at 4pm. Please bring all

necessary documentation with you for a formal interview with myself and my colleague Sarah Andrews.

Please let us know if this is convenient for you.

Kind regards

Geoff Fiske, HR Manager

▶ **Your reply**

Geoff,

Re: *Application for Software Developer

*Thanks very much for your invitation to *attend an interview on Monday 21st at 4pm. This is very *convenient as I will be in the area on Monday for another interview.

I look forward to meeting you and your *colleague Sarah Andrews and will bring all the relevant *documentation with me.

*Kind regards

Chris Hawkins

This email is in a similar tone and style and includes some words and phrases used in the incoming email. This might be a good opportunity to look back through your own emails and notice your style, tone and language. How have you matched the emails of your colleagues and friends?

TELEPHONE RAPPORT

Obviously the same rules apply when speaking on the telephone. If the interviewer is chatty and expansive then it is fine to give examples and anecdotes. However, if the interviewer is somewhat short and economical with words do not be too chatty. Keep your examples and lengthy sentences down to keep in rapport. Notice the tone of voice and pace of the conversation and match that too. Naturally all this needs to be done subtly and without appearing too obvious. However, it is a fact that people who know each other well or family members are often quite naturally in tune with each other. As humans we adapt to the behaviour of those around us quite naturally.

If you observe people in the workplace or at home you will notice they are generally in rapport with each other.

Marketing yourself

How do you 'market' yourself to a potential employer?

Having decided what kind of job you would like and chosen the companies or areas you would like to work in, the first action is to focus on your skills and knowledge in this market.

- What specific experience do you have that matches this work area or company's profile?

- If you look at the job description, what can you find in your own work history that is particularly relevant or matches a specific skill?

- Can you think of some examples? (Such as a project you took part in or something you did/contributed to that worked well.)

- What key selling points can you focus on? (Yes, you are effectively selling your skills and experience.)

Try this model:

SAO: Solution, Action, Outcome

Imagine you found yourself with a problem and you managed to solve it. Outline the solution you thought of, then what actions you took and how you managed to obtain a successful result. Here are few examples from both practical trades to management positions.

Recently I gave a workshop for 14 young apprentices who were going for their first interview. I asked them to give me examples of the SAO model. At first they found it difficult to come up with examples; however, after several people had given their ideas, the floodgates opened. Here are just three of their examples:

▶ A joiner

When I was fitting a kitchen for a customer I noticed that the floor was very uneven and that the cupboards wouldn't fit properly.

Solution: I thought about how I could make the cupboards fit so that they didn't move around and the worktop was even. Then I realized that by fitting adjustable feet to the cupboards I could counteract the uneven floor.

Action: I made the feet so that they could be adjusted on three settings.

Outcome: The cupboards fitted well and could be moved into place creating a flush work surface.

▶ IT assistant

The reporting system in the office was muddled and there didn't seem to be a real system.

Solution: I decided to ask for all reports to be filed every Friday and for each worker to sign off on a list before leaving.

Action: I sent out a memo to all workers outlining the system and how they needed to sign off every Friday as they passed my desk.

Outcome: This system worked very well and we were able to put a follow-up system in place so that reports were acted on promptly. It was very efficient.

▶ Welder

There was a task I was given where I wasn't sure if I could carry out the job on my own, as I thought it sounded like a two-man job.

Solution: I decided to call my supervisor to explain the situation and get his views.

Action: We agreed to bring in another member of the crew to assist me.

Outcome: This meant the job could be completed efficiently and on time. The customer was very happy.

These are all excellent examples of how you can market yourself effectively to your future employer. Giving examples of how you have shown initiative and found solutions to problems shows your ability to think on your feet.

According to recent research employers are looking for someone with the ability to:

▶ **think on their feet** and to perform well under pressure

▶ **demonstrate their ability** through examples and brief anecdotes or stories

▶ **initiate** or start something of value (a project, an idea, a new technique or process, etc.)

▶ **work in a team** and be able to demonstrate how they have successfully done so

▶ **be self-motivated** to stay focused, finish what they started and meet deadlines.

Therefore, it makes sense to focus on the criteria above and prepare a list or mind map in order to match your skills and experience accordingly.

Focus points

The main points to remember from this chapter are:

✳ Review what you have done in the past and what you can offer in future.

✳ You must research the company you want to work for and the role.

✳ How you communicate, and how well you communicate, makes all the difference.

✳ Your main task is to market yourself to your potential employer.

Next step

In the next chapter you will take your research and begin to identify the kind of role you are suited to. You will understand what skills and knowledge are transferable. You will also begin to develop rapport with others and get yourself in the right mindset so you can move forward.

Preparation

In this chapter you will discover:

- *Your ideal role*
- *How to mentally prepare for the job application process*
- *How to put yourself in the position of others*

So what needs to happen next in the process? You want a job which gives you satisfaction, allows you to pay your bills and motivates you to get up!

Look at you

Think again about what you are really good at. If you are not sure, ask your family or colleagues how they see you – ask them to write down your strengths and qualities, no matter how trivial they seem. This all helps to boost your confidence.

Try it now: Ideal role

Imagine yourself in your ideal role or one you found on the internet or the newspapers you scanned (this may seem far off but you need to take the first steps). Now think about the kind of tasks and skills you may need for this role. What skills are transferable from a previous job or how can you made the skills fit this particular role?

Case study

Simon was feeling disheartened. He had lost his job at a local IT company where he had been working as a web designer for five years. He wanted to stay in the IT industry but needed a challenge. He didn't know how to look for a job or prepare for an interview as his current job was his first and had been offered to him via a family friend. He felt his skills needed freshening up and that he did not have much to offer a prospective employer. He felt, in his words, 'unsure of who I am on this journey'.

So we dug a little deeper to discover what kind of person was going on this journey. I asked him a 'clean' question: 'And when you are unsure and feeling unprepared, what kind of *you* would you like to be on this journey?' He replied that he would like to be similar to his colleague who was confident and had good technical skills. I followed this by asking: 'And when *you* are confident and have good technical skills, what kind of confident is that?' (emphasizing the 'you').

This prompted him to imagine what kind of confidence *he* might need to support him as this would be different from his colleague: 'Oh I think

I would be confident, a bit like when I do off-road mountain biking. I am really in the zone and feeling a rush of excitement.'

Then I asked: 'And when you are in the zone and feeling a rush of excitement is there anything else about confident like that?'

'Yes, it's powerful and gives me a 'can do' attitude'

As we developed this biking metaphor he began to understand how he could use this for feeling more confident during the job search. He also developed a metaphor for when his confidence took a knock, as he had often fallen off his bike and then been able to get back on, even if this was tough. Keeping this visual in mind he was able to continue to the next phase of the journey.

We started by going through his five-year job history with the company and he made a record of all the tasks and projects he had been involved with. He was surprised to see quite a list of past projects. In answer to some incisive questions he was able to see how many skills he had gained. As he developed his responses he was amazed at the knowledge he had picked up over the years. It had seemed quite hard to voice these skills at the start but as he thought back more came to light. He began to see where his skills might fit into a new role in IT. He identified areas where he would like training to update his knowledge. On the internet he found a local enterprise agency that was offering free courses in SEO (search engine optimization) that were of great interest.

What is your job history? Have you been in a job but are now looking to find something new or different? Are you returning to work after some time away? Or are you looking for your first position?

Try it now: More questions

Try these questions:

* When you imagined yourself in your ideal job (in the previous chapter), how did it feel? (Stop and really feel it.)
* What were you thinking and seeing in front of you? (Stop reading and think for a moment.)
* What roles/jobs/tasks have you had that you really enjoyed? (Cast your mind back and visualize them.)
* What kind of 'you' are you when you work really well? (Create a metaphor like Simon above – When I work really well I'm like...)
* What kind of confident 'you' would you like to be?
* What roles/tasks would you really enjoy? (Imagine and make a note of them now.)
* What makes them enjoyable or rewarding? (Add this to your notes.)
* When you think about your past job/position what tasks/projects/ roles did you do well? When you are working well, you are like... what? Keep going back to your metaphor and develop it with 'What kind of [your words] is that...'. (Stop for a few moments and note down or make a mind-map of your own work history; if this is your first job think about your roles at school/college or university.)

Focus on any recent success, no matter how small. Think about any direct evidence/testimonials/references you may have from your previous college/colleagues/boss/associates/customers, etc.

If you do not have any, ask for them – it is surprising how willing people are to write testimonials if you only have the courage to ask.

Keep at the positive aspects of the job search like a dog with a bone and do not allow your mind to focus on any negative aspects. If they come floating in, just notice them and bat them gently away. Imagine how hard it is to swim upstream and how easy it is to allow the positive flow to take you downstream towards your goal.

You need a clear mind and a positive 'go for it' approach in order to succeed. Then begin to prepare your own questions and consider the questions that may come up from the interviewer. Write them down. Go over them several times until they become second nature to you.

Mental preparation for interview

All top sports people and successful business people prepare mentally for the challenges they face.

Think about the following:

▶ What do I bring to this occasion? (e.g. knowledge to share, transferable skills, positive attitude, etc.)

▶ What am I leaving behind? (e.g. the bad weather, the unhelpful chatter, the terrible traffic.)

▶ What are my expectations for this interview? Do I want to be right/faultless or do I want to relax and enjoy the moment and give my best?

▶ What can I tell myself now so that this interview goes as well as I expect?

Case study

Colin had received very negative feedback years ago which affected his confidence.

He was asked to present a report to the whole class, his hands began to sweat and he felt physically sick. It didn't help when he was told to 'get on with it' and not to be 'so stupid'.

This had a very damaging effect on him as, after several similar experiences, he felt he really was 'stupid' and of course he has, in his mind, plenty of evidence to prove this. As time went on he gained more self-respect but always had these 'voices' in his head. As a result he found he was not able to assert himself in day-to-day situations and eventually lost his job. After joining a local speakers' club and receiving coaching to boost his confidence, he realized that the 'evidence' proving his 'stupidity' was no longer there. He could see that he could in fact contribute well to a team and had excellent transferable skills. He was delighted to relate a very positive experience some time later. He had been into his local job centre and applied for a job where he felt he could really succeed. He came across in a very convincing fashion and got the position he was looking for. He is now more able to face his fears and work through the barriers to effective communication.

Make a concerted effort to put the past and all its negative experiences behind you. Be aware that you *can* change the patterns and give yourself a chance to succeed if you choose to. Invest some time on the techniques in this book and see the results for yourself.

Key idea

The key to success is to use all the senses to prepare and rehearse, particularly when you are out of a job and want to appear confident.

In Chapter 1 we explored the use of Clean Language and metaphor to help you to think about your new job and what it would be like. We will now take this one step further. This will enable you to use your senses to project yourself into the new job. It will enhance those feelings of self-belief and motivation, and train your mind to prepare for that job you enjoy.

Try it now: Clean Language questions

Consider this question again and read the sample answers that follow:

❊ When you are working at your best in a job you enjoy **it** would be **like** ... what?

Sample answers taken from clients:

1 It would be like a well-oiled machine where each part had an important function and performed it well. It would be easy and not need constant attention.

2 It would be like working in a comfortable hotel where you were made to feel welcome, where you had your own duties but where people were on hand to help you when needed.

3 It would be fast paced and exciting, like watching a sporting event. There would always be a challenge and you'd feel part of something energetic and invigorating. Your ideas would be listened to and you'd have opportunities for promotion.

Then follow this by asking:

❊ And when you are in a job you enjoy and working at your best **you** are like ... what?

The same people answered by developing their original metaphors as follows:

1 Umm well I'd need to be part of the well-oiled machine and performing my tasks to the best of my ability. I would be learning and have the confidence to ask questions if I needed to. I'd have to take time to understand the methods and ways of working and not get sidetracked.

2 I'd be like a bird building its nest, fetching and carrying but feeling I was building my career from small beginnings. I would like to be useful and resourceful and work well as part of the team.

3 I guess I'd be like a skier, well prepared both mentally and physically and up for the challenge. I would need to be willing to share ideas and listen to those with more knowledge and experience. I would need to be patient at first both with myself and others!

Try those two questions for yourself again, now that you have seen the examples. This will project you into the working world and prompt you to think about the job itself and your role in it. Take time to think this through to really benefit from this technique.

Try it now: Timeline

A very useful NLP technique for really connecting to a desired outcome is the time line. First we will look at a way of understanding where you see/hear/experience things in terms of time and space.

Imagine a time when you had a really good meal (perhaps five to six years ago). Then think of a time when you had a good meal in the past week. Now imagine a meal that you might have in the future. When you think about the meal in the past, where is it in terms of space around you? For example, many people see the past behind them (we often say of bad past experiences, 'Oh I have put that all behind me'). However, not everyone sees the past behind them. For example, I see it to my left, my current situation as directly in front of me and my future to my right.

This may take a while to work through, as we are not used to thinking about our past, present and future in spatial terms. If you don't find this easy, just move on.

When considering the timeline for a new job, ask yourself the following questions:

✳ When you have that new job, what will you see, hear, and feel? (Really experience all your senses as if you were actually there in your new job.)
✳ And what's important about that? (Imagine what emotions, ideas, surroundings are most important for you when you are enjoying your job.)

Then ask yourself again, 'What's important about that?' until you have all the answers you need. This is a way of finding out what your true values are and what you need for your job to be satisfying and enjoyable. When you find your new job it is important that you keep the position for as long as possible, as this boosts your confidence. There is no point in taking a job and then having to leave after only a short time, feeling you didn't fit in or the job wasn't right. Get it right the first time and then you will be rewarded with a job you enjoy!

Take a look at what you have written or drawn as being important for you in your next job. Feel and experience those emotions, ideas and surroundings as if they were already happening, as if you already had that job and were working in it. I suggest you put this book down and take time to really visualize this for a few minutes. Give yourself the luxury of being in that job you enjoy for a while.

By doing this you are training your brain to be prepared for your new job. You are beginning to allow your thoughts to influence your subconscious mind, to lead you to a more fulfilling role, and you are accepting that you can influence your own future journey.

Now take another look at all you have been noticing about your new job. Increase the colours and positive feelings, intensify the emotions and take yourself on a rich and colourful journey. See the surroundings, hear the people and watch what is going on around you.

Now hear your own voice as if it were describing this picture/situation to someone else. You can speak out loud or record it so that you can play it back at any time. This can be very helpful in training your mind to take on your own true values and what is important to you. Once again your mind will start to accept that this is where you need to be and begin to support you with a positive mindset. While doing this you have been accessing your own memories of positive emotions and thoughts from your past knowledge and/or experiences. You have re-created them to imagine your new job and projected them into the future. You have, in effect, created your own timeline. If you received some thoughts or emotions from a less than positive source, focus only on those that are positive. Put aside those that are unhelpful as they have no place in your new mindset. (You are not denying that they existed but merely not allowing them to influence you – your choice.)

Let's return to those pictures and feelings you had when thinking about your ideal job. When you created the timeline you imagined your future role and you noticed where your past was on that line. Now draw that imaginary line on the floor and notice again where the past, present and future lie. Step off that line for a moment and look into the future. Now walk to where your new job is on that line – walk only to where you feel comfortable and connect with all you desire in your new job. Really feel as if you are there and experiencing that sense of achievement. You have found your job, passed the interview and now you are there. Just take time to experience that feeling and live that dream like a fizzy buzz filling your body and mind.

Now look back towards the present and either take a piece of paper or draw a diagram to plan your steps from the future to the present. Step back from the timeline (the meta position) and observe from outside any other actions or points you need to plan in order to reach that job you enjoy.

Next, walk back to your present position on the timeline. Record and notice those steps that will take you to your new job. Notice how you feel, what you are thinking and hearing in your head, and stay focused and above all positive and motivated. In order to gain real clarity and to imbed those action steps and plans, I suggest you stop and repeat this exercise again. Perhaps you can involve a friend or colleague to help you or to do this together for mutual support.

Planning your interview strategy

What follows are general guidelines for planning and organizing your interview strategy.

Try it now: Planning can be fun

If you like diagrams or pictures when planning, take a large piece of paper (or use the computer) and draw a mind map or spider graph. Plot your skills, knowledge, experience, ideas and job-related hobbies so that you can see them clearly in front of you. Highlight specific areas. You may need several thought maps or graphs until you are satisfied that they contain all the vital elements.

If you prefer to plan with lists, write down your skills, knowledge, experience, ideas and hobbies. Then re-order them into various sections relevant to your application.

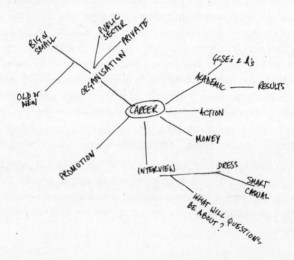

Start with your introduction and a little background relevant to this position. Choose three key points to focus on with regard to skills and knowledge. Follow up with all the questions – both theirs and yours – and decide what your final words will be as you leave.

TIMING

It is vital to ensure you do not overrun or are too brief and miss an opportunity.

If, for example, you only have 30 minutes for the interview, calculate: five minutes for introducing yourself, twenty for the main part of the interview and five for your own questions and conclusions.

Once the preparation and planning are in place, the last of the three Ps remains – just practise your visualization and affirmations, practise your own questions and those you may receive, and practise your desired outcome by using positive words to describe and really 'be part' of it.

PAUSES AND SILENCE

Being comfortable with silence is a great asset. All those 'um's and 'ah's can be reduced if you are able to 'be' with the silence. All interviewers need time to absorb what you said, so learn to pause before you dive into the next question. Take your time to answer their questions and think about what you want to say. Unlike you they have not heard about your skills and experience before and need time to process it.

One great NLP technique is the use of perceptual positions to get into the shoes of the other person. When preparing for interview this can be really helpful and also takes away a lot of the fear.

Try it now: Reflection

Think for a moment of a previous interview or personal experience where the communication didn't go as well as you would have liked. Then take some time to ask yourself these questions:

* How do you think the other person/interviewer felt when you said...?
* How did you feel/think when the person/interviewer asked you...?

The method outlined below will really help you to expand your thinking and see things from the interviewer's perspective.

PERCEPTUAL POSITIONS

(This is best done with a trained coach for best effect. However, reading this through and really imagining yourself in the situation will help you to gain a greater understanding.)

Perceptual positions involves looking at a situation from your perspective, an other's perspective and an observer's perspective.

▶ **Self**

If you have a past interview experience, do the following:

▶ Imagine and visualize the interview situation.

▶ Close your eyes and really 'see' the situation unfolding.

▶ Then think carefully about what you said and the other person's reaction.

▶ Really hear what you said, what they said, and how you felt at the time.

▶ If you find it helpful, say *your own words* aloud as you said them at the time.

Then for a future interview experience do the following:

▶ Imagine what you are trying to achieve.

▶ What are your objectives and main points to get across at this interview?

▶ What is important to you in this situation?

- What kind of person is the interviewer? (If you are not sure, just imagine.)

- What are your thoughts and feeling towards them?

- What possible differences in beliefs, values or culture might arise?

- What is your own preferred style of working? (Activist, reflector, pragmatist, theorist, creative/ideas, big picture, detailed, team player, etc.)

- What can you do to ensure the relationship is as good as it can be from your side?

▶ The other (interviewer)

In this part of the process you will be putting yourself in the shoes of the interviewer. This is so you can really get a sense of who they are and the kind of feelings you may have towards them. Many misunderstandings occur because people do not take time to see things from another's point of view. (Even if you haven't met them yet, use either an interviewer you experienced in the past, or how you imagine them to be.)

Visualize yourself being in the interviewer's body now, take on their stance (or imagine it) and really be as they are as far as possible. This works best when you sit in another chair to take on *their* character and demeanour. Now *as the interviewer,* take a long look at yourself and how you are. See the interaction and imagine the conversation from *the interviewer's* point of view. (Really become that interviewer, using their words and thoughts.)

- What are your objectives as the interviewer? What outcomes do you want?

- What is important for you (the interviewer) in this situation?

- What do you think/feel about the candidate in front of you? (Be honest – this is *you* the interviewer is talking about!)

- Pay attention to what you see, what you hear and how it feels.

▶ You can also say the words of the *interviewer* as they said them at the time (or as you imagine they may in the interview).

▶ What insights and new information have you had being the interviewer?

▶ The observer

Imagine the conversation again: this time you are a *neutral observer*. In this role you are aiming to hover above the situation. Aim to be dispassionate and objective.

View the conversation from a distance and watch the interaction between those two people (you as SELF and the interviewer as OTHER) as they were in a previous interview (or how you imagine them to be in future).

▶ Really hear the words and feel the emotion between SELF and OTHER.

▶ Ask yourself if there is anything you can learn from observing them from above and really hearing and seeing them interact.

Then ask yourself:

▶ What did you notice as the non-judgemental observer that could help this communication/interview next time?

▶ What questions/observations/comments were helpful/unhelpful?

▶ What was done to create a good rapport between them?

▶ As observer, how comfortable did you feel in this situation?

▶ What did you notice that may have contributed to the outcome of this interview/interaction?

▶ What advice would you give as the neutral observer?

Now, back as SELF, ask:

▶ Is there anything you could do differently to turn this situation around or to prepare better/well for your interview in light of these thoughts?

▶ What action can you now take to ensure the interview goes smoothly and that you can really create a good relationship?

Now try repeating the perceptual positions again to see if any other thoughts or feelings emerge. You may be surprised at the way this process sheds light on the interviewer and your own reactions and feelings when facing them. If you have not yet met your interviewer, this exercise can still evoke feeling and thoughts that will help you in creating the right atmosphere. It will show you areas where you may have 'your buttons pressed' and which areas of your interview technique you need to develop.

Preparing for an interview

Interviews vary and the format can change from informal to very formal. They can last for one hour or one to two days depending on the company or organization.

There are three keys areas to consider wherever your interview is being held:

1 the company or organization

2 you as the candidate

3 the interview itself.

Think about each stage of the interview and how you would like to respond and interact with the interviewer(s).

How do you announce yourself as you enter the room?

▶ 'Hello, my name is [your name] I am here for an interview with [name of the company or interviewer].'

▶ 'Good morning/afternoon, my name is [your name]. Pleased to meet you.'

What do you say if you are asked a question and don't know the answer?

▶ 'I am afraid I don't know but I am willing to...' [Insert what is appropriate.]

▶ 'I haven't had any experience of that but I am sure I could learn.'

▶ 'I haven't come across that before, could you explain please?'

- 'I don't know the answer to that I'm afraid, could you clarify?'

- 'I'm not sure I understand you correctly, do you mean...?'

- 'I'm not sure I know the answer, so could you expand on that for me please?'

- 'I'm sorry I don't know.'

Bear in mind that it is always better to say you don't know than to bluff your way through. You will always be found out in the end. (For more on questions, see Chapter 5.)

What do you say when leaving the interview?

- 'Thank you for this opportunity, I look forward to hearing from you.'

- 'Thank you very much, it was nice meeting you.'

Even if you feel the interview did not go very well, keep your head up, your voice steady and thank them as you leave.

What do you say when facing the interview panel?

- Say why you want the job and tell them what your strengths are, e.g. 'I am very interested in [aspect of the job] and I feel that my strengths as a [mention your particular strength/skill] will make a useful contribution to this role.'

▶ Let them know specifically what you have achieved to date in a similar role (if relevant), e.g. 'In my previous job I was particularly good at [your strengths in a team or during a specific task].'

▶ Express your personal and professional goals and values. Speak openly and honestly about them and what plans you have to achieve them, e.g. 'I would love to achieve my goal of [e.g. team leader] and I enjoy [supporting others and seeing them grow]. I feel this role would allow me to [extend my communication skills and build on my existing qualifications].'

▶ Explain that you can provide references if required, e.g. 'I have two or three up-to-date references, and my referees are happy to be contacted.'

If you need to do a presentation, note down the key points you want to include. These may be, among others:

▶ Your knowledge of the company (brief overview): 2 minutes

▶ How and why you would fit into the organization: 2 minutes

▶ Your particular strengths and experience with examples: 6 minutes

(Timings will need to be checked. Above is a rough guide for a ten-minute presentation.)

If you have worked for this type of company before, what experience will you be bringing to this role? Be very clear and specific. If this is a new role, what transferable skills do you have? Often a role outside of work can contribute to your knowledge and skills. It is very useful for companies to hear about *all* your experience, knowledge and skills, not just those that are role related.

PREPARING YOUR QUESTIONS
Remember that:

1 Your voice tone and body language are very important – take your lead from the interviewer(s).

2 Speak clearly and keep eye contact with the person who has asked the question.

3 Breathe and listen carefully to the responses to your questions.

   a Think about what you need to know and practise delivering all the questions you can think of.

   b Base your questions on your research and knowledge of the company.

(For more on questions, see Chapter 5.)

BEFORE THE INTERVIEW

▶ Ensure that any thoughts that are interfering with your being totally focused drift out of the window (traffic, disagreements, problems, work and so on).

▶ Focus on your preparation and bring yourself fully into the room.

▶ Notice what is going on around you and show interest.

▶ Concentrate on your deep breathing to keep calm – one breath out to release the tension, one breath in to gain energy.

Give yourself some positive affirmations before entering the room. Remember these are positive statements in the present, such as:

▶ I am well prepared and have my questions ready.

▶ I have sufficient knowledge and skills to do this job.

▶ I am able to remain focused and relaxed.

▶ I can learn what I don't know.

▶ I am smart and suitably dressed for the role.

▶ I keep good eye contact and sit upright.

▶ I answer questions with due consideration and enthusiasm.

▶ I feel confident and know I can do well.

REMEMBER WHAT YOU HAVE PREPARED

So, you have prepared what you want to say, your questions and thoughts – how do you remember it all?

You can:

▶ Use notes or cards to jog your memory.

▶ Use highlighted areas of your job description or CV.

▶ Rely on your memory.

▶ A combination of the above.

Let's have a look at all these methods in more detail.

Having cards or notes is fine, provided you are organized. It is better to have a maximum of three cards with:

▶ the main areas of your skills, knowledge and experience relative to the position

▶ your own questions for the interviewer

▶ your parting words as you leave the room.

(The latter is very important as you want to leave a good impression.)

One very useful tip is to recognize that as soon as you believe you can succeed at interview, you will be able to. It is all about *trusting in your own ability*. Just trust that all will be well and you will deliver in your own natural style. It is not advisable to copy someone else. Watching successful interviews on the internet can be very beneficial, but remain true to your own style. Start to visualize yourself giving a successful interview. Practise giving yourself these positive affirmations to eliminate the negative self-speak. These statements may not be true just yet, but by repeating them you are enhancing your self-belief and boosting your confidence.

Get into the habit of repeating these statements daily, and add your own:

▶ I am able to speak confidently at interview.

▶ I can ask intelligent questions.

▶ I have relevant skills and knowledge.

▶ I trust my own ability and preparation.

▶ I am ready give a good interview, naturally, in my own style.

! Focus points

The main points to remember from this chapter are:

✳ Mental preparation and a positive mindset are crucial.

✳ Plan your interview strategy.

✳ Look at the interview from different points of view so you have a clearer idea of how you come across.

✳ Prepare thoroughly and remember what you have prepared.

→ Next step

You will now take a look at how you come across to others and how to present yourself in the best possible light: your use of voice, gestures and stress patterns and how to pause and use the silence to think clearly during the interview. You will also discover how to cut the negative chatter that prevents you obtaining interview success.

Part Two

During the Interview

Presentation and Personal Image

In this chapter you will discover:

- *The importance of speaking clearly and of your body language*
- *How to show your authority*
- *The options for presentations*
- *Why to address technical issues before you start*

Presenting yourself

DICTION AND PROJECTION

In order to project your voice and be confident, you need good breathing and relaxation techniques (see Chapter 5). Go back to the breathing exercise and notice how much more you can project with good breath control. Good singers practise breathing techniques every day, so do public speakers. If you are giving an interview presentation, so do you! After the breathing exercises you need to work on your projection. It is possible that you will be speaking to a panel and will need to project to the other side of the room.

Try it now: Projection

Take yourself to a secluded space where you will not be overheard. This exercise can really help your projection and diction:

Stand at the back of the room and look at a point on the opposite wall. Imagine you are speaking to it.

Stand with your feet a little apart and with your shoulders down and relaxed.

Keep your chin level and your throat free.

Say the following one after the other, being clear to pronounce the consonants (these are not 'a, e, i, o, u'– which are the vowels): 'Ship ahoy!' 'Help Help!' 'Look out!' Stand back!' Bounce the sound off the wall in front of you.

Now put your hands on your diaphragm breathe out, in, out, in – then repeat the above again. Remember to expand the diaphragm and keep the mouth and throat relaxed and open. The sound should be low and mellow not high and forced.

Now on one breath (breathe in) try the vowels: a, e, i, o, u.

Make them hit the wall. If you are out of breath, then you need to practise your breathing exercises. The muscles of the diaphragm are like your fingers when you start to play the piano – stiff and unused to the new position. With practice you will be able to project and breathe with ease.

Practise every day.

Think about your breathing and don't forget to pause and allow the words to flow naturally. Allow yourself to exclaim and concentrate on the vowels this time: 'Oh what!' 'No!' 'Well!' 'Really!' 'Oh heavens!' 'You can't be serious!'

This is meant to help you explore your vocal variety and to be fun as well.

Now repeat the consonants: 'Ship ahoy!' 'Help Help!' 'Look out!' 'Stand back!'

Ideally do this in front of a mirror to check if you are really opening your mouth and breathing correctly. This needs to be done in a relaxed position so you may like to begin each time with the breathing and relaxation exercise.

These exercises will give you confidence and extend your vocal variety. Notice when you rehearse your questions how some words are stressed for emphasis. Listen to the radio and notice the stress patterns. Ideally record yourself asking and answering the questions in Chapter 5. You will be able to correct your pace if it's too fast or slow. Notice how your voice is projected.

Posture is vital to voice tone and volume. So when you walk in for your presentation, stand with your feet slightly apart. Feel your body as if it were being pulled gently upwards by a silver thread. Hold your head lightly on your shoulders and relax into a firm stance keeping your shoulders down.

GESTURES
The very best way to make an impact at an interview presentation is to be as natural as possible. Gestures can add great value but they need to be sincere and really appropriate for the occasion.

Some tips on making effective gestures:

▶ Make the gesture suit the words.

▶ *Feel* the gesture, don't just do it.

▶ Make the gestures bigger than usual – convincing.

▶ Smooth, well-timed gestures have more impact.

Remember this
It is important to be authentic as interviewers can pick up on gestures that do not align with what you are saying.

Good planning and preparation will enable you to create fluid gestures. Put time aside to think about where your gestures will be most appropriate. Use them sparingly for greater impact.

For example, during your presentation you may be describing one of the people you 'invited for dinner'. The person may have been someone who had given you a very strong handshake that hurt and you may 'shake your hand' to demonstrate this. This can add a little humour, particularly if it is brief and appropriate to the situation.

CUT THE CHATTER

You have the power to decide which thoughts you allow to occupy your mind. To a large extent you determine your success by the thoughts and emotions you choose to accept or discard. This is often hard to come to terms with. Sometimes it is very difficult to change patterns of behaviour you have drifted through life with. You feel comfortable with them, they are 'old friends' and although they may be bad for you, you hang on to them staying in your own comfort zone.

So how can you turn out the old chatter that no longer serves you ('I'll dry up', 'I'll make a fool of myself', 'I have never been able to speak in public') and start to introduce the new images and thoughts?

▶ **Creating new habits**

If you are patient and replace the old chatter with 'I'll give this a try', 'everyone makes mistakes', 'I'll learn as I go', you will slowly begin to trust yourself. You will suddenly become aware that you *do* have some control over what success you have at interview *by what you pay attention to in the present*. Take action now!

As you have noticed, NLP concentrates on supporting you to make small adjustments to the way you think and behave. Refuse to be concerned with regrets and guilt feelings: tell yourself that fear can be replaced with quiet confidence. Fear is only possible without knowledge and trust in your abilities. Imagine those times when you have been good at or succeeded at something, remember them and shut out the voices that tell you: 'You will fail', 'You can't do this', 'You're no good', 'What if they laugh at you?' etc.

Try it now: Positive messages

Remember, if you think of yellow cars that's what you'll see – yellow cars. If you think about problems that's what you'll notice – problems!

What positive messages are you going to replace your old chatter with?

Take a few moments to think about the following before continuing:

✻ What are your current unhelpful chatter or thoughts around presenting?
✻ What could you replace those with?

Make the old voices laughable and take on the new ones. No one is like you or has *your* stories to tell. You may think that what you have to say is not interesting (those voices again!), but everyone has experiences that interest others.

EYE CONTACT

It is important to engage your panel/audience with individual eye contact. You will most likely be facing a panel of three or four people. It will be easy to ensure you give them all a few seconds of eye contact as you speak. However, some companies require you to present to your competitors so the audience can be larger. Select a few friendly faces you notice and speak to them. Turn your whole body in their direction – this is particularly important if an interviewer asks you a question. Take your time and if you notice someone is considering your reply, avoid rushing to the next point.

BODY LANGUAGE

Your body language is vital and will show whether you are confident. Standing tall and giving a firm handshake is the first element. Then when you are sitting facing the panel or interviewer, remain relaxed but alert and remember to smile!

PACE

When you are nervous, the instinct is to rush your words, so practise your questions and answers with a friend or colleague. Learn to build in pauses and vary your pace during the interview or presentation. Watch for the interviewer's body language and notice when they are considering your answer or a response to your question. Give them space to breathe and take your time before jumping to the next slide.

Key idea: Pauses

Pauses are the 'time to think' parts of a conversation and really create a feeling of ease in the relationship. Consider the questions that arise and really give space to the meaning of each one. Pause before you respond and allow yourself time for a breath or two. This shows the interviewer you are confident and in control. People whose preference is auditory or kinaesthetic need this space to take in what you are saying more than those of a visual tendency. Be alert to the pace of readers when presenting slides and let them read before you continue to speak.

VOICE TONE

You will use your voice in different ways for different situations. In an interview it is vital to use variety and to inject your voice with enthusiasm and energy. If we take the pauses and pace into consideration, then voice tone is equally important. The stress you put on different words, the way you lower your voice at key moments can all have an impact. When you enter the room you will be using a neutral tone to introduce yourself and settle in. Later when you are being asked questions it is useful to be more energetic and stress key words. You will need to show your motivation for the role and be enthusiastic about the company you hope to work for. When you ask your own questions, your voice needs to be firm and slightly lower in tone. You will be showing interest and genuine curiosity about the role.

If you use vocal variety in your interview and presentations, then you will appeal to all the different types/styles. Matching the voice tone and pace of the interviewer can also be a useful strategy, but should be used with care and for genuine rapport building.

GETTING CENTRED AND GROUNDED

Five to ten minutes before you are due to give your presentation:

▶ take a few deep breaths in and out from the diaphragm (base of the rib cage)

- focus your mind on the room where you are waiting

- look around with awareness and 'centre' yourself in the here and now

- bat away the chatter and intrusive thoughts

- breathe and just 'be' for a few moments.

Then think about the following:

- What do I bring to this presentation? (e.g. a brief anecdote, knowledge to share, a useful piece of information.)

- What am I leaving behind? (e.g. the bad weather, the unhelpful chatter, the terrible traffic.)

- What are my expectations at this interview? Do I want to be right/faultless or do I want to enjoy the experience and give it my best?

- What can I tell myself now so that this presentation/interview is as I would like it?

Creating your personal image

When you turn up at interview you will be judged as soon as you enter the room, so the first few minutes are crucial. Think about the occasions when you have met people for the first time. You noticed their appearance and their attitude. You may have had thoughts about the way they were dressed or if they had nice eyes. You made unconscious judgements about them before they even said a word.

Before you enter the room, think about the mood you want to create. Will the interview be relaxed and informal or will you be giving a powerful presentation to a panel? You can send out very different messages with subtle variances in the way you dress. It is useful to consider what image you are presenting. If you stand in front of your mirror you will have a totally different image of yourself compared with people viewing you from a distance during a presentation.

Try it now: Dressing up

Stand in front of your mirror in the outfit you will be wearing complete with any accessories. Then stand back as far away as the interviewer(s) will be. Notice if your style has the same impact.

A colleague told this story at a recent interview where she had given a brief presentation.

> I dressed in a smart suit as I was presenting to the panel for a job in a law firm. However, I wanted to add a touch of colour so I wore a bright-red shirt with a high collar under my jacket. After the presentation I was told that this had 'shone' in the lights and had actually distracted from my message. I realized that I had not taken into account the impact that the red shirt had from a distance or under the bright lights.

On this occasion red earrings and a strong red necklace may have been a better choice. On a man, a smart suit with a brightly coloured tie may have the same result.

Subtle use of colour can add a dash of energy and excitement to a dark suit. Don't be afraid to use it but think carefully about the impact each item will have. If you wear a strongly patterned tie, suit or blouse it may look great on a one-to-one basis but can easily distract at a distance. For a formal setting, darker plain colours are usually more effective. You do not want to take the attention away from your skills and experience. In a less formal setting, lighter colours can be worn but stick to plain materials or very subtle patterns.

SHOWING YOUR AUTHORITY

This will depend on the occasion and the mood you want to create.

In a *formal* setting, women will appear more authoritative when wearing the following:

▶ a suit either with trousers or a skirt to the knee

▶ a long straight skirt of a darker shade and in a plain material

▶ a formal blouse (where the cleavage is not too apparent)

In a more *informal* setting, women can opt to:

- leave a blouse open at the neck and a jacket undone
- wear simple jewellery to add a little sparkle and a dash of colour.

Men will appear more formal when wearing:

- a dark blue, black or pinstriped suit as is usual in the business world
- a brown or grey suit (for slightly less formal occasions).

For an informal occasion, go for:

- a smart/casual jacket and trousers
- plain or lightly striped shirts (suitable for most occasions)
- a plain or subtly patterned tie (or no tie).

Remember this

An upright confident posture is your main asset when presenting yourself for interview.

A good rule of thumb is to dress just a little smarter than your interviewer. For example, if most people are in open-necked shirts or blouses and no jackets, slip on a jacket for your interview and take it off when mingling afterwards, if this is an all-day affair. Add touches of colour to a formal suit to create an element of surprise, but avoid loud statements that will detract from your delivery. You want to be remembered for what your words conveyed not for a fashion statement.

If you respect your interviewer by dressing well, creating rapport will be easier. Your image speaks volumes and it only takes a little time to consider how you come across. This is always time well spent, and if you don't have a long mirror, visit a local store that has one!

Another concern people have is about being too tall or too short. Shorter women have the advantage of high heels but men can also buy blocked shoes to increase height. However, it is not really that important. If you stand tall and exude confidence, you will not need heels as your attitude will carry you through. If you are tall, celebrate the fact and avoid stooping or leaning forward.

Interview tools

SKYPE/TELEPHONE

Some initial interviews are conducted via telephone or Skype. The same good preparation is needed but naturally you will be listening even more carefully. You will need to research the company in the same way and prepare your own questions. You will not be able to use eye contact or body language so your voice and vocal variety is more where your focus will be. Apart from the usual interview questions on past experience, job roles and abilities, you may be asked to discuss a case study or solve a problem with the interviewer. Questions such as 'what would you do if...?' or 'what action would you take in this situation?' may arise.

FACTUAL INFORMATION

NLP makes extensive use of stories and metaphor. People tend to think in metaphor and use it to illustrate how they are feeling. These are metaphors often heard in the workplace:

- nose to the grindstone.

- banging my head against a brick wall.

- getting caught up in the detail.

- work's getting on top of me.

- getting to the bottom of it.

- out of the woods.

- I've cracked it! ball park figure.

- I've squared it with him.

- getting down to the nitty gritty/nuts and bolts.

- like water off a duck's back, etc.

If you tell a story or use metaphor, even factual information can be entertaining. Think of the situations around your facts. What story can you weave into the dry material? How can you get the panel involved? Nothing surpasses interaction as a way to engage, teach or persuade listeners. Ask hypothetical questions such as:

▶ Do you know how much time I saved just by using this strategy?

▶ Have you ever considered how this might work for you?

Asking this kind of questions (those that do not necessarily need an answer) helps to engage people and gets them thinking. At an interview presentation this needs careful planning and when used thoughtfully can be very effective.

PRESENTATIONS USING POWERPOINT

The PowerPoint presentation has taken over from slides and it can greatly enhance a presentation, or it can kill it!

Here are some tips when using PowerPoint presentations at interview which incorporate NLP techniques. First, it is important to remember that it is not *what* you say but *how* you say it that really counts. People tend to select with their emotions and if they feel you are reaching out to them they are more likely to view your presentation favourably. The meaning of your presentation is reflected in the response you get.

Key idea

Getting feedback on how you come across can be invaluable. Get someone you know well to give you an honest appraisal of how you come across on all the following points. This could mean the difference in your getting a job or not! It could also be the reason why you have not been chosen in the past, so be aware.

▶ **Further tips for presentations**

▶ Use images to reinforce numeric data.

▶ Summarize the key message of the slide at the top.

▶ Leave plenty of white space on each slide.

▶ Use bullet points not complete sentences – less is more.

- Alternate colours on tables to improve visibility.
- The message is more important than your logo/name.
- Keep your logo/name in the same place on each slide.
- Keep each slide to a minimum of three points.
- Increase attention with full-screen images.
- Keep fonts and overall design consistent.
- Use either photos or clip art – not both.
- Tell a story with a beginning, middle and logical conclusion.
- Space out your information for a smooth professional presentation.
- The image they will take home is your last one – make it the best.

There are some great online resources for adding effects or images to enhance your PowerPoint presentations. For example, you can upload a photo and then change it into a pencil sketch. On another website you can key in a quote or a signature and transform it into any script you fancy. You can even copy text onto an image of your choice.

For example, if your presentation was illustrating how you demonstrate your ability to manage your time, you could copy and paste key phrases onto a clock face. However, at interview keep the humour low key and use sparingly.

Visit the following and have some fun: www.redkid.net/generator/bumper. There are many more, so search for 'web generator' and see what comes up.

Remember this

One or two surprising slides can really make a difference to a dull presentation. Obviously too many can kill it, so keep a balance and enjoy.

USING A FLIP CHART

This is a great visual aid. You can use a flip chart to add spontaneous drawings or diagrams to emphasize a point. Just keep the following in mind:

- Use thick blue or black pens.

- Write large letters/diagrams – ideally not capitals.

- Make sure there is plenty of white space.

- Do not crowd the sheets with information.

- Bullet points are clear and easy to read.

If you can prepare these sheets in advance, all the better – then you will not have to turn your back on your audience.

TECHNICAL EQUIPMENT

Pitfalls to avoid when using technical equipment:

- Always check your equipment and any hired items at least one hour before you begin the setting up process.

- Setting up always takes longer than you expect so plan in advance.

- Make sure you have a contact at the venue who knows the equipment.

- If the PowerPoint presentation doesn't work check the following (as obvious as they seem, each one is vital):

  ▷ You used the correct sequence when turning on the equipment.

  ▷ Both the laptop and the projector are plugged in and turned on.

  ▷ You have put in the correct password (if necessary).

  ▷ If you are using a memory stick, check that it is inserted correctly.

  ▷ The projector has the cap removed.

  ▷ The screen is placed so that the image can be projected effectively.

  ▷ If the image is too small, move the projector further back from the screen.

  ▷ If too large, move it towards the screen.

▷ If the image is slanted, adjust the feet/foot on the underside of the projector.

▷ If the image is too low, place a book underneath the projector.

▷ If too high, use a lower table or adjust the foot on the underside of the projector.

▷ If you are using a remote control, make sure it is attached correctly and that the connection is not loose.

Do not be afraid to ask for technical help *in advance*. You do not want to have to stop in the middle of your presentation if it goes wrong. It is not good to blame the technician half way through if you haven't checked the equipment!

USING A MICROPHONE

Most interview presentations are without a microphone. However, if you are in room with poor acoustics you may be offered one. Be aware of the following:

▶ Microphones are temperamental and need checking and re-checking beforehand. Avoid banging the microphone or and blowing into it to see if it works as that can cause damage.

▶ Just say 'testing' a couple of times and get the technician to adjust the levels for you. Have a small signal that tells the technician to raise or lower the levels.

▶ Never speak with your lips on the microphone as this muffles the sound. Hold a hand-held microphone just below your mouth and speak normally. When turning your head move the microphone as you speak unless it is fixed. Make sure when you make a gesture that your face is not too far from the microphone. The best way to do this is to pause when making the movement so your words are not lost.

▶ Most annoying for an interview panel is when the speaker has pages of notes rustling into the microphone. Put your notes on cards that are easily laid onto the lectern and do not rustle. Once again, when turning the page/card, pause for a moment before you speak.

Oh, and remember you have a microphone. It is surprising how many presenters forget to turn it on before speaking! Using a microphone can be really helpful. It is definitely worth learning how to do it efficiently for maximum impact.

Focus points

The main points to remember from this chapter are:

✲ Present yourself well – clothes, posture, composure and presentation techniques all make a difference.

✲ Take a few minutes before a presentation to gather yourself and think positive.

✲ Test the technology before the interview or presentation starts.

Next step

In the following chapter you will focus on interview questions. What questions are common? What specific questions can you expect? What questions should you prepare for? How can you calm your nerves when asked difficult questions? All will be revealed!

Coping Strategies and Questions

In this chapter you will discover:

- ► *How to face those 'what ifs'*
- ► *How breathing techniques can help*
- ► *What you could ask your interviewer(s)*
- ► *Ways to approach challenging questions*

In this chapter, we will cover a few of the 'what ifs' and look at some of the communication skills and strategies you may find helpful during the interview.

What if...?

Here are some of the 'what ifs' I have heard from my own coaching clients.

What if:

▶ there is someone better than I am for the job?

▶ I don't have the right skills/knowledge?

▶ I can't answer the interview questions?

▶ I don't know what to ask at interview?

Let's look at numbers one and two in the context of a case study as they have cropped up several times.

Case study

Lucy was coming back to work after having her first child. She had previously worked in a media company as a production assistant but felt that she lacked up-to-date knowledge. The industry had moved on and she thought there would be people more skilled/knowledgeable than her.

(Note: This coaching session was carried out using Clean Language. Each time I ask a question it begins with 'and'; this is so the stream of consciousness is not interrupted. The words then feel like a continuous thought process. It enables the facilitator to stay out of the way and allows the speaker to stay in their own thoughts and emotions with less interference. By mirroring the actual words of the speaker they 'hear' their own thoughts and this means that they are able to reach their own conclusions faster and more effectively.)

(C: Coach, L: Lucy)

My first question for Lucy was:

C: And when there may be more skilled/knowledgeable applicants than yourself what would you like to have happen? (eliciting a positive desired outcome)

(Lucy thought for a few moments and we sat in silence so she had time to think. Then she reflected.)

L: I would like to feel confident that my own skills and knowledge were as good as others and that I wouldn't fail at the interview stage.

C: And when you feel confident that your skills and knowledge are as good and you wouldn't fail at the interview stage, then what happens?

L: Oh then I wouldn't worry about getting out there and I'd be actively applying for jobs.

C: And when you feel confident, is there anything else about confident like that?

L: Yes, I feel rusty and am not sure my skills and knowledge are up to date.

C: And what needs to happen for you to feel confident and sure your skills and knowledge are up to date?

L: I really need to investigate what employers are looking for and then retrain. Then I would feel more confident to actively apply for jobs.

(The session then continued as we explored the kind of training and what would enable her to feel more confident.)

C: And when you are confident and actively applying for jobs, what kind of jobs are they?

L: Well, they'd still be media related but interesting and motivating. They'd involve people I like working with.

C: And when they are interesting and motivating and involve people you like working with, is there anything else about media jobs that are interesting and motivating?

(Again Lucy need time to think about the question and took several moments to reflect.)

L: Yes, I was thinking back to my last job and feeling that it didn't really interest me towards the end. I hadn't realized that till now. This time round I want to find something that is more rewarding.

C: And when it's more rewarding, what kind of rewarding is that?

L: Umm, it's a step up from my last job to make it more motivating and I guess that's where I was feeling my skills and knowledge may need updating.

(Notice that Lucy has now got a metaphor for more motivating – 'a step up'.)

C: And when your skills and knowledge need updating, and it's a 'step up', what kind of 'step up' is that?

L: Oh maybe a step up from assistant producer to actually being the producer – wow that's sounds quite motivating!

C: And that sounds motivating, and it's a step up, and more rewarding, and people you enjoy working with, and updating skills and knowledge, and when all of that is there anything else about a step up?

(Note: It is part of Clean Language to reflect back what a person has said so they can hear their own thought process and check if this is really what they want. Often people are not aware of their own thought patterns or words.)

L: Yes, I need to find out what skills and knowledge I need to take that step up. It would really be great to be a producer and also my salary would be better. Now we have a family that's important to me. I need to call a few people and get hold of a few job specs so I have an idea of what is needed.

C: And when you know what is needed for the step up then what happens?

L: Then I can enrol on a course and there would be people there doing the same thing so I would gain confidence too.

C: And you would enrol on a course and gain confidence and there'd be other people and is there anything else about step up like that?

L: Well I suppose I would start to feel less concerned that others were more skilled or knowledgeable than I was. I would feel supported and be learning and that would give me a boost to start looking for a new job.

C: And feel less concerned and feel supported and be learning and give you a boost and whereabouts is 'feel supported' like that?

L: Umm, it's kind of wrapped around me and keeping me safe.

C: And it's wrapped around you, keeping you safe and when you are safe, that's safe like … what?

L: Oh safe like a warm soft blanket that I can take when I feel anxious or need support I suppose.

C: And safe and around you and support (using her words) and what needs to happen next?

L: Ah well I need to do some research and find out what courses are available and then select some prospective jobs.

C: And can you do that?

L: Yes I can, as now I feel safer and more motivated to get on with it!

C: And will you do that?

L: Yes, I can start on the research this weekend.

This is a shortened version of the coaching session showing key areas as an example. At the end of this session Lucy drew a picture representation of her metaphor 'step up' and how she would use the 'soft blanket as a support' – she found it helpful to keep this with her to stay safe, motivated and focused.

As in the case study above, start to focus on what you need to do to ensure you are well prepared and your skills are up to date. You can never know what the skills of other interviewees are or how much knowledge they have. So it is wasted energy to focus on them. The only person you can work on and improve is you.

Find out what is needed for the jobs you are interested in. If you have been out of the workplace for a while, take one of the many free courses offered by local enterprise agencies and business clubs. As Lucy realized, there will also be other people in the same position as you and this can be very supportive.

So now we will turn to the other two 'what ifs'

WHAT IF I CAN'T ANSWER THE INTERVIEW QUESTIONS?

If you find you can't answer the interview questions there are a couple of things you can do. We can assume you have researched the company before the interview and you have asked yourself in advance all the questions you think may come up. If you still find the answers elude you, then be totally honest.

Case study

Let's take a look at Jessica when she was suddenly at a loss for an answer at her interview.

(C: Coach, J: Jessica)

C: So what happened?

J: Oh well, I just lost it! I couldn't think of the list of values they had on their website and they asked me if I knew them. I had read them but I couldn't remember.

C: So what would you have said if you hadn't lost it do you think?

J: Umm, well, I suppose I would have said exactly what had happened. That I had read them but that I wasn't able to recall them.

C: Yes, as you know we have discussed this and when you panic the brain freezes and then you really can't remember. In this case it is best to just take a breath and be totally honest, as you were. If you are calm then often the brain will kick in and provide you with your answer.

J: Yes, the other thing I thought of was to tell them I was feeling a bit nervous and just ask them to prompt me with a couple.

C: Yes, that's fine as most interviewers know that you are nervous.

J: Yes, they were quite supportive and I think honesty was definitely the best policy in this case.

So when you are stuck for an answer:

▶ Be honest.

▶ Take a breath and pause for a couple of minutes to see if the answer comes to you (this also looks as if you are considering their questions which is good).

▶ Ask the interviewer to clarify what they asked as you are not sure of the question.

▶ Just say simply that you do not know (sometimes, if this refers to a skill or technique, you can add that you are willing to learn, if this is appropriate).

Here are some examples:

▶ I am afraid I don't know but I am willing to ... [insert what is appropriate].

- I haven't had any experience of that but I am sure I could learn.

- I haven't come across that before. Could you explain please?

- I don't know answer to that I'm afraid. Could you clarify?

- I'm not sure I understand you correctly. Do you mean...?

- I'm not sure I know the answer, so could you expand on that for me please?

- I'm sorry, I don't know.

Bear in mind that it is always better to say you don't know than to bluff your way through. You will always be found out in the end.

WHAT IF I DON'T KNOW WHAT TO ASK AT INTERVIEW?

This is often something that my own clients find difficult. However, these days with internet research it is easy to find out a great deal about the companies where you are applying to work.

Let's think for a moment about the kind of questions you might like to know. What did you visualize as your working environment? What kind of people were they and how did they interact? What tasks were you allocated and how much support did you receive?

You may not have gone into so much detail but nonetheless these are the beginnings of useful questions.

Breathing techniques

Keep yourself calm by taking your time. Use deep breathing techniques to steady your nerves. If you breathe correctly from the diaphragm this will get rid of the jitters and the wobbly feelings. This kind of breathing counteracts the panic you feel and allows the body to relax. You can train yourself to respond to fear not with tension but with relaxation. The diaphragm is located at the bottom of your rib cage. Place your hands on your diaphragm with the fingers facing each other. You will feel a little space at the bottom of your ribcage.

Speak clearly and keep eye contact. Breathe between questions and listen carefully to the responses to your own questions. Think about what you need to know and practise delivering all the questions you can think of. Base your questions on your research and knowledge of the company. Keep yourself calm by taking your time.

Your own questions

You will be asked if you have any questions of your own during the interview. Having a few ready is always helpful. However, keep them brief. As a rule of thumb, asking four to five questions is about right. Assuming you have already had the job specification, here are some general questions you may like to ask during your interview. They will not always be appropriate, but will give you a general idea. Select those that feel the most appropriate and leave the rest.

▶ How many people are employed in this section/department/area/company?

▶ What kind of projects/areas/tasks will I be involved in?

- Who will I be reporting to?

- Do the teams/employees work collaboratively?

- How are employees supported?

- Are there any training courses or employee resources available?

- How do you see the company's future?

- What makes this a good company/firm/organization to work for?

- Do you supply a uniform? (If appropriate.)

Consider asking the following, if the details are not in the job description, or terms and conditions:

- What hours will I be required to work?

- Do you have a canteen/supply meals or vouchers?

- What holidays am I entitled to?

- What salary can I expect to receive?

- How is this paid?

- Is there a bonus system?

- Will I be working on commission or for a salary? (Some sales jobs are based on commission, so check this out.)

Now you have gained some ideas, begin to formulize your own questions. What do you need to know about this company/job? Having done your research and read the job description, what are the key areas you'd like to hear about?

Ask yourself some questions so that you are clear about what you need to know. For example, if your question is, 'Who will I be working for/with?' then ask yourself:

- What kind of person/team would I like to work for?

- What would enable me to work well with them?

- Where/how do I work best?

- What is that like ... when I'm working at my best?

- What am I feeling, thinking, noticing, hearing when I am working at my best?

Keep asking these kinds of questions until you are clear about what you need, and what environment you can work best in.

After looking through your own questions, put about five of them in order of priority and get rid of the rest.

Their questions

Particularly think about how to deal positively with any challenging questions that you may be asked during the interview, such as:

- What do you know about the company and its products/ services?

- What made you apply for a job in this organization specifically?

- That's interesting, can you expand on that?

- In your CV you mention you have experience in [X]. How would you apply your experience to this role?

- Tell me more about your knowledge of [X]?

- What makes you particularly suited for this job?

- What makes you interested in this company specifically?

- What past experience and skills can you bring to this job?

- Can you give me some examples of a problem you have solved?

- Are you able to take the initiative? How can you demonstrate that?

- What are your main strengths and weaknesses?

- How do you see yourself in this role?

- What attracts you to this job?

- There will be a lot of [travelling/stress/teamwork, etc.] involved – how will you deal with that?

There are many different questions that can be posed in job interviews. This book does not attempt to provide all of them. Instead you will gain an understanding of the type of questions that determine successful interviews. These will also prompt your own questions and help you to prepare for them in advance. Remember there are no tough questions, only those you haven't prepared for! Use the visualization techniques you developed from the previous chapters. Really 'see' yourself in the interview room and use all your senses.

Then go through 'their' questions above and prepare your answers. Do this in a way that suits your learning style.

Remember this

Neglecting to prepare will make the difference between succeeding or failing at interview.

Try it now: Visualization

Even if the room and the people are different to those you imagine, you will feel more confident and prepared if you do this visualization.

* Imagine being in the interview room. Look at the style and the layout of the furniture.
* See the people (one or more?) and think about what they may look like.
* Hear the sounds that might be audible (telephone, paper, doors, etc.).
* Smell the room and imagine how that might be.
* Feel your emotions and notice your reactions to being in the interview room – stay calm and breathe!

Notice your body and the sensations that are running through you and *practise staying relaxed*.

This is a way to really prepare well so you can stay in control on the day.

Answering challenging questions

When you know the kind of questions you will be asked it is easier to prepare. This is a sure way to give yourself the edge over the competition.

▶ What made you apply for this job?

If you have researched well and you know specifically what interested you in the position, this question will be straightforward. You may answer:

> Well, although this is my first job, I am very interested in [X].

If possible, also say specifically why you were interested.

If you have experience or knowledge of the job you can answer:

> Well, as I used to work in [X] this job is ideal. I have skills and knowledge in [Y] and I really enjoyed doing [XX project/role/task] in my previous job.

Even if the job is boring, not exactly what you wanted or you are not particularly interested, try to remain positive and enthusiastic. It is your attitude as well as your aptitude that will determine the outcome of your interview.

▶ How good are your organizational skills?

When you first read about the role you may have thought that you had no organizational skills at all. However, everyone has organized something in their lives. Look at your hobbies and interests to see what you have organized. Maybe you were part of a team but you still had a role to play in making that event or situation successful. Dig deep and find what you have done in your personal and professional life to add value to your interview responses.

If you have very little experience, be truthful as it never pays to lie at interviews.

Your answer could be something like:

> My organizational skills have not been tested too much. I have been helping my local club with their fundraising events though, and I am able to manage my own time quite well.

Find something you are good at and let the interviewer know, even if you feel it is not very significant. It may make all the difference.

If you have had experience and can draw on specific examples, use them to illustrate when and for what projects/tasks you have used your organizational skills.

▶ What have been your most successful achievements to date?

Again you may think your achievements are not worth mentioning. Remember to think positive. This is your chance to show the interviewer what you can do.

You may have won a prize:

> Well last year I won an award for the presentation I gave to our regional teams.

Were you a member of a successful team or organization? What hobbies or interests do you have? You may have done something for charity:

> Actually I belong to a local charity and I do their books for them and help them organize events.

In your previous working life, what positions have you held and what responsibilities have you taken on? What did you achieve along the way? This could be anything from promotion to taking on more responsibility for a project. It might have been helping your colleagues out of a tricky situation, to fundraising or organizing an event. Think back to those times where you were successful and what you did to contribute to that success.

Particularly think about how to deal positively with any challenging questions that you may be asked during the interview. You could stop for a moment to take a breath and visualize your past working life and the experiences you had. Note down the key moments and your part in them.

If this is your first job then be honest and let them know you are willing to learn and train for additional skills. If your hobbies are related in any way, see if you can find some relevant transferable skills.

Perhaps you are keen on a particular sport and this job is sales related. Sport and sales are both quite competitive so you understand how sales are important to keep ahead of your competitors. If you really pay attention to your own skills and knowledge, there will often be parallels to draw.

▶ Other questions

There may be more incisive questions such as:

- ▶ Tell us how you would deal with X.

- ▶ How would you go about planning for Y?

- ▶ What experience have you had managing teams/people/ conflict and so on?

- ▶ Are you an activist or a reflector?

- ▶ How would you organize X?

- ▶ How would you deal with aggressive/disruptive behaviour?

- ▶ How good are your organizational skills?

- ▶ What makes you an effective manager/team player/sales assistant/worker? How do you know?

- ▶ What makes a good manager/team player/service provider/ assistant ... in your opinion?

In the final phase you may be faced with the following questions:

- ▶ Have you read the terms and conditions of employment?

- ▶ Are there any areas of the job description you would like to discuss?

- ▶ Are you happy with the hours/terms and conditions/holiday arrangements?

- ▶ Would you be prepared to work overtime?

- ▶ Are you prepared to work shifts/flexitime?

- ▶ If you are granted this position, what salary would you be looking for?

- ▶ Would you accept this job on a commission only basis?

- Is there anything else you would like to know?

- You may be called for a second interview. Would this be convenient on...?

- Can you provide us with references? Please leave their contact details.

SCENARIO-BASED QUESTIONS

When applying for senior roles, you will come across scenario-based questions. These test your ability to deal with real situations or challenges that arise in the workplace. This is to see how you would behave in a pressured environment or when faced with a tricky situation. They are usually posed with:

- What would you do if...?

- What action would you take if...?

- What would your reaction be to...?

- How can you demonstrate X or Y?

- If this problem arose [they describe it], how would you solve it?

Do:

- keep calm

- breathe from your diaphragm

- remember you have answers prepared

- pause and think before responding

- take your time and trust you will come up with something.

When responding, be sure to highlight your areas of expertise, your key strengths and behaviours. You may be confronted with several tasks and need to prioritize them. There may be tasks you need to delegate and others where you need to make a quick decision. Whatever you are faced with, remain calm and breathe deeply. The more you practise, the better you will become when confronted with unexpected scenarios.

Often there are questions around your own knowledge and skills you have outlined in your CV. For example:

> We notice you have skills in XX – can you tell us about a recent project you have been involved in where these skills have been particularly useful?

Or:

> You mention you have good knowledge of XX – can you explain how this has helped you to create a strategy or plan for a particular project or situation?

Do not dwell on the details of the projects but show *how* and with *what skills* you were able to solve the issue/situation. The interviewer is looking for your behaviour and the use of your knowledge and skills in this scenario, so focus on that and keep your response brief.

There can also be questions where the interviewer asks about aspects of your job that may have gone wrong. This is to test your behaviour when times are tough and things are not going according to plan. For example:

> Can you think of a situation where things may not have gone the way you expected? How did you deal with that?

Again, preparation for these questions can really take the sting out of the situation. Think back to a time where this might have occurred. You will have not always been successful, but it is the way you dealt with it that the interviewer is looking for. Give a very brief overview of the situation and focus on the way you handled it and what you did that was positive and solution focused.

Once again visualizing can really help. Take yourself into these various scenarios and imagine how you would think and feel. Rehearse each one so that when you are faced with these more challenging questions your answers become natural and flowing.

THE WAY YOU COMMUNICATE

Pay attention to your own language when you respond to questions. The use of 'but' can be distracting when you are in an interview situation. The word tends to conjure up negative images and be unhelpful. Interviewers will generally hear and remember what you say *after* the 'but' more clearly than what you say *before* it. Let's look at an example:

> **Statement 1:** I was able to develop a really effective sales strategy for the project by acting on what our clients had requested, *but* my delegation of the tasks was not so successful.

The interviewer will most likely focus on the unsuccessful delegation of the tasks.

> **Statement 2:** My delegation of the tasks was not so successful, *yet* I was able to develop a really effective sales strategy for the project by acting on what our clients had requested.

The interviewer will now focus on what you did effectively and the first part of the statement will be noticed less. Also replacing the word 'but' with 'yet' has placed a more positive emphasis on the statement.

Look again at more examples to illustrate the poor effect of 'but':

> I hope to be able to illustrate this with an example, *but* it may not be relevant.

The interviewer hears that your example will not be relevant, so they switch off.

> It may not be relevant, *yet* I hope to illustrate this with an example.

The interviewer hears that you will illustrate this with an example.

Another aspect of language to be mindful of is the leading or particularly negative question that may cause you to feel pressured.

The interviewer may ask: What aspects of your personality do you feel cause difficulties in the workplace?

This kind of leading question is taking you down the path towards a negative response. It is best to respond honestly. To prepare for such a question let's take some examples:

> One aspect of my personality is that I can be quite curt and offhand when I'm under pressure. This can cause others to feel I am rude or disinterested. (So far you have been open and answered the question – now you need to turn it around.)

> However, I know this about me and I have worked on my behaviour, as this is not helpful to either to me or my colleagues. (You have now revealed a more positive aspect of your character.)

> How do you manage the situation if you come up against difficult or resistant colleagues?

Again if you have prepared your answer you will be in a position to answer this with confidence. One example could be:

> I listen to their side of the story and then I try to stick to the facts of the situation. I provide examples of how I would like things done and how the company operates.

Or:

> In my experience people are generally less resistant if you listen to their views with respect. If they are refusing to take a course of action I always try to find out the reasons for their resistance. Often it is a matter of clarity and greater understanding.

A word of warning; if you have experienced difficult colleagues and really dislike them, avoid including them in your example as you will show your dislike by your facial expression and voice tone!

▶ More advanced interviews

Applying for a position where you will be managing other people or taking on a leadership role may need other considerations. Often you will be asked to attend a whole-day interview and give a short presentation.

Questions may arise to test your personal style or the way you interact with others.

Case study

James is one of many servicemen who have recently retired from active service. He wanted to use his many skills in an interesting and challenging position. Having worked for the Air Force, he decided to apply for a job with one of the civilian airlines as a pilot. He was asked to attend an interview lasting all day.

The first part was an interview in front of a panel. The second was a scenario-based interview assessing leadership and decision-making skills. Finally, there was a group interview where candidates had to give a five-to-seven-minute speech.

During the day James was mingling with other candidates and senior company employees. He had studied the company background and was fairly sure they were looking for outgoing people who would be able to interact well with their customers. James made sure that he spoke to as many of the candidates as possible. He made a real effort to create rapport with individuals and applied his listening skills to good effect. During the panel interview, he had prepared relevant questions and his extensive research had enabled him to answer their questions.

For the group interview candidates were given two questions to think about during the day:

✳ If you could have lunch with three people, living or dead, who would you choose and why?
✳ What made you choose this company to work for?

At the end of the day all candidates were asked to give their answers to the questions in a five-to-seven-minute speech. This was in front of all the other candidates and senior employees. James applied all the public speaking techniques he had learned as a member of a toastmasters speakers' group.

He had only a little time to plan, but made a few notes as the day progressed. He used the following:

✳ breathing and relaxation techniques to calm his nerves
✳ a few affirmations so he felt confident
✳ positive thinking to make sure he was passionate and enthusiastic
✳ a strong statement for his beginning
✳ interesting stories about the people he had chosen to join him for lunch

Extensive research plays a vital part in succeeding at all-day interviews, as does displaying confidence and mingling with people you have only just met. If you would like to read more about speaking well in public, my book *Make a Great Speech* is a good place to start.

When you rehearse these more challenging questions, notice these small changes in approach and language as they can bring about a different mindset.

Remember this

Plan, prepare and practise, and keep in mind some of the core NLP principles:

* Focus on what you want to achieve and ensure your objectives are clear.
* Do not waste energy by dwelling on problems – be solution focused.
* Work with all your senses and really notice where your preferences lie.
* Engage others to support you in this journey as far as possible.

If you want to change your approach to your job search and/or improve your interview skills, you will need to invest time and energy for that change to happen – be patient!

Focus points

The main points to remember from this chapter are:

* Plan, prepare and practise.
* Prepare some questions for your interviewer(s) in advance.
* Deep breathing can help calm your nerves.
* You may be asked challenging questions, but preparation will help you answer them effectively.

Next step

The importance of both mental and physical rehearsal cannot be under-estimated. All successful people prepare well for the different challenges they face. You will discover tips and techniques to help you do the same. This will give you the edge over your competitors.

NLP Techniques

In this chapter you will discover:

▶ *The importance of rehearsal*
▶ *How to use metaphor as an anchor*
▶ *How to create rapport with your interviewer(s) and other candidates*

Mental rehearsal

After trying visualization and seeing yourself in the situation as it could be, the next step is mental rehearsal. This is a way of embedding positive thoughts in your subconscious. These thoughts will program your brain to view the situation in a good light. They will strengthen your resolve and underline your key skills. Think of these positive thoughts as true or almost true. Familiarize your mind with things as you would like them to be. You are probably used to doing the reverse, as negative thoughts are more common. Bear in mind that negative thoughts just serve to pull you down, and resolve to banish them with positive mental rehearsal.

Try it now: Mental rehearsal

Using a voice recorder, a computer or note pad, describe yourself in positive terms as you would ideally be, look and sound in the interview room. Use the present tense where you can.

For example:

> I enter the room feeling relaxed and confident. I have done my research and I feel I can answer any questions that may come up. I am able to smile, speak enthusiastically and give people eye contact. I look smart and have taken care over my appearance. I am listening well to what is being said and responding appropriately.

Use your own words and do not be concerned if you do not feel these statements are entirely accurate just yet. The more you repeat these phrases to yourself the more you will start to embed them. A top athlete before key events such as the Olympics will mentally rehearse in this way to gain confidence and exceed their targets on a regular basis.

Case study

Lynda was at a career crossroads. She had carved out an excellent career in nursing and was now a highly regarded and experienced senior ward manager. Lynda had always felt that being a Matron was her ideal job and that she was well qualified to further her NHS career and step into the role.

The requirement

After two unsuccessful interview attempts, Lynda was feeling demoralized and even questioning whether she was following the right career path. She decided that when the right opportunity came along that she would invest in some professional interview skills coaching to help her overcome her interview 'demons'.

The coaching process

Lynda was asked to recall what went through her head on the day of the previous interviews. Despite being such a positive and outgoing person who was very active in amateur dramatics and performed regularly on stage, she was all at sea when it came to interviews. She even admitted to 'freezing' in her last interview. Lynda's language was full of self-doubt and she showed a lack of confidence. She had limiting beliefs around her interview technique and surprisingly her ability to do the job as matron.

If this was what was occurring on the day of the interview, it was hardly surprising she was not successful. She was also really concerned how her family would react if she didn't get the job as she didn't want to let them down. Hardly a positive word uttered so far! She admitted to coming across this way in her interviews, which would have planted doubts in the panel's mind whether she was right for the job.

When asked how her colleagues would describe her she suddenly came to life:

> They call me a star because they say I am passionate about what I do and deliver the best care for my patients. They say I am brilliant at my job and have great knowledge which I share with them. Also, the way I go about my job and go the extra mile, motivates them so they see me as an excellent role model.

Lynda was clearly underselling herself, her capabilities and achievements! Her problems were all being caused by her mindset, limiting beliefs, fear of being asked difficult situational questions, her modesty and the domino effect of repeated rejections.

The solution/cure

Steve then coached Lynda to focus on the following:

1 Getting into the zone: what made her smile and feel good about herself?

Her response: 'My family and especially my kids. Last time they drew me a picture which said 'mummy Matron' and I let them down.'

Lynda now focused on visualizing the following scenario:

She had been told she had got the job and was seeing herself in the matron's uniform and telling her family she was 'mummy matron'. Also, she was encouraged to think about her kids when entering the interview to make her smile and feel good about herself.

2 Overcoming her modesty and use of 'I'

Having seen the power of her response when asked what her colleagues say about her, Lynda was asked to practise confidently using third-party endorsement' in her answers to direct questions such as 'tell me about yourself' or 'tell me about your achievements'.

For example: 'my colleagues say', 'my boss always says' and to try to imagine them saying the words rather than feeling she was 'blowing her own trumpet'!

3 Aiming to 'intrigue not inform': use of compelling examples when answering difficult questions

Lynda tended to ramble then run out of steam and freeze. She was asked to think about framing her answers in a similar way to the TV news by giving compelling headlines and then adding some short punchy specific examples using positive, confident language to reinforce her answers and show her competency. Also, when faced with a difficult question she should take a deep breath and then think about her kids. In this way she could reframe her thinking and answer the question naturally and positively rather than freeze, as before.

The result

Lynda was able to hone her technique, overcome self-doubts and completely reframe her mindset so she could only see herself being successful and in that Matron's uniform. Sure enough this is exactly what happened and she blew away the interview panel, 'nailed the interview' and landed her dream job. She has since been commended for her performance, which was the icing on the cake!

What Lynda said made the difference

* Getting into the zone and smiling by thinking about her kids.
* Using third-party endorsement: she commented that she could almost see and hear the people she was talking about when she gave her answers, which gave her a massive confidence boost and helped her answers flow.
* Focusing on only positives and positive language, so not giving the interview panel any reason to doubt her.

Case study kindly contributed by Steve Preston,
www.steveprestonthecareercatalyst.com

Essentially Lynda's preparation for the interview, including practice, made her feel comfortable tackling both the direct and difficult situational questions, plus it increased her overall confidence and self-belief. She came to realize that it was only her who had doubted herself!

As you will have noticed from this case study, it is useful to mentally rehearse and also to see yourself as other close friends might see you. This is what is meant by third-party endorsement.

Try it now: Friend feedback

What would your closest friend or a supportive relative say about you? Perhaps imagining them saying your strengths and qualities out loud would help you to hear how good you are. Ask them to tell you your strengths and what skills you bring to the table. Notice how they praise you and where they think you are competent and knowledgeable.

The most powerful way to really allow this technique to be effective is to visualize it. With this method you will be totally involved, experiencing it with all the senses and in full colour. When you think of the people involved in your third-party endorsement really bring them into the room with you and 'hear' what they have to say.

The same will apply to when you are sitting in your own room and imagining the interview room. Feel how confident and relaxed you are. Breathe slowly to control your nerves. Really 'see' the interviewer as you imagine them and notice how calm and in control you feel. Use all of your senses for this exercise. Really hear the sound of your own voice (record it if you do not know!) and hear the sound of the chairs being moved in the room. Smell the room as you imagine it might be – perhaps there is coffee being made so smell that too. Feel the door handle as you enter and the chair as you sit down. Enhancing your awareness by using all your senses will allow you to immerse yourself in the experience and will stimulate your subconscious. You will be effectively training your mind to experience the interview in positive terms.

Then, as an observer 'see' yourself in the interview room. Experience how you are listening well and answering the interviewer's questions with ease. Notice your body language and the gestures you are making. Watch your enthusiasm and the easy flow of conversation. Listen (still as an observer) to the tone of your voice and the way you interact with the interviewer. Feel how you reveal or hide your emotions and feel the energy flowing between you and the interviewer. Watch as you enter and leave the room with confidence. Repeat this until it feels second nature and your confidence has returned.

Note down what you have noticed from the 'observer' position and if you would change or do anything differently as a result. You may have 'noticed' you were speaking softly or slowly so next time you can 'turn up the volume' or pick up speed in your mental rehearsal. Remember you are in control of what you rehearse for!

I have often heard people say that things are not possible because of X or Y but that can often be the result of negative assumptions. Unfortunately, we are faced with so many negative messages in a day. If you train your mind to accept positive thoughts and visualization some things will become more possible, such as finding a job.

The following is an example of how these techniques can work:

A few years ago I was a member of the local toastmasters public-speaking clubs. Unexpectedly I won the evaluation competition in my local area and then also the district competition. This meant that I had to speak at national level and I found this very daunting. There would be about 500 people and I had never spoken to so many people face to face before. I used the techniques above to help me to focus on what I did well and not on the audience and expert speakers that would be there! I imagined myself walking onto the stage with confidence, feeling calm and hearing the audience applause before and after I delivered my speech. I gave myself a kind of 'energy spot' to feel and walk into for the enthusiastic parts of the speech. Then I used another 'calm spot' to feel and step back into for the pauses and less dynamic areas of the speech. I watched from the 'observer' position as I delivered my speech clearly and enthusiastically using the stage and interacting with my audience. Imagining this clear visualization in my head over several weeks in preparation made a huge difference to the way I felt. I was delighted when I came third out of 20 finalists.

Go back to visualizing as yourself (rather than as the observer). Now you are actually in the interview room, imagine different scenarios. For example, imagine different types of people, attitudes and behaviours. Imagine you are under pressure to answer something you are not familiar with or you face a tricky question. Note down the different areas where you may feel challenged.

Now see yourself handling these scenarios easily and being calm and in control. Rehearse all the possible situations that could cause you anxiety. Picture yourself being at ease in any situation. Notice how decisively you are able to deal with them. Feel and hear the strength of your voice as you answer the questions. Experience the confidence and smile from within as the interview progresses. Use breathing techniques to enable you to 'keep calm and carry on'.

Then go back to the colourful and confident you who is now in control of each situation. Bring all your senses into play and think through the scenarios, feel your body and how it is reacting, hear all that is happening in the interview room. Recall those positive images visualize the confident 'you'. Rehearse as if you were really there with the interviewer in the room. Only if you rehearse these worst case scenarios will you be ready to face them in the real interview. Taking yourself through this process will remove the fear as you will have trained yourself to react appropriately.

Feel yourself calm and in control and able to handle anything that is thrown at you. Remember you will need to repeat this a few times to really embed the mindset you need for success.

Use of metaphor as an anchor

In NLP, anchors are used very effectively as a reference point for a particular experience. As we have seen previously metaphors can help to create a visual picture of you when you are working at your best. This can really help to keep you focused and feeling motivated.

After you have done your mental rehearsal and you are beginning to feel more confident, choose an anchor.

An anchor can be likened to a ship in a harbour: it is safe and protected, and easy to access. You use anchors in your life without realizing it every day. Sometimes these anchors are negative: for example, in the past you might have been bullied at work by a manager. Now, perhaps without consciously realizing why, you have a fear that all managers could be bullies. You can replace these negative anchors with more helpful and inspiring thoughts and feelings.

When you are looking for a job it can be helpful to ask yourself what really motivates you? This could be a variety of factors, for example fulfilment, money, security, sense of self-worth, confidence, being with others, etc. Take some time to think this through and decide what your main motivation is for finding a good job. Then think about what that gives you. Let's take Mandy as an example in the following case study.

Case study

Mandy needed a job urgently as she was a single mum and had a two-year-old boy who she had enrolled at a local nursery. She liked working with others and needed the money. These were her two main reasons for finding a job. This is a brief summary of the second coaching session we had.

(M: Mandy, C: Coach)

C: You want to work with others and you need the money. So what kind of work is that when you are working with others and you need money?

M: Umm, I think I'd like to work in an office of some kind as I am good at organizing, and I like working with computers and social media, that kind of thing.

C: And work in an office and need money. Is there anything else about money?

M: Yes I would like to make at least £16,000 a year to cover my child care and expenses.

C: And £16,000 a year. And what kind of office is that?

M: I think I'd like to work in a law firm or in the courts as I did that a couple of years ago.

C: And work with a law firm or in the courts and £16,000 a year to cover child care and expenses. And what needs to happen next?

M: I need to take a look online for job websites ... umm that feels a bit scary!

C: And that feels scary, what kind of scary is that?

M: A really tight feeling in my stomach.

C: And whereabouts in your stomach is that tight feeling?

M: Here. (She points to an area around her navel.)

C: And when tight feeling is there anything else about that tight feeling there. (I point to her navel.)

M: Yes, I don't like it and it feels uncomfortable.

C: And what happens just before you get this tight feeling in your stomach ... there?

M: I think about the interview and how I will probably fluff it!

*C: And so what would you **like to think** about the interview?*

M: I'd like to think it would go well and that I would feel confident ... but I don't!

C: And you'd like to think it would go well and you'd feel confident and what kind of confident is that?

M: Oh like my brother who always seems to get what he wants!

C: And like your brother and what happens just before you are confident like your brother?

M: (thinks for a minute) Umm ... well he often says he 'sees' himself in a particular role or situation.

C: And work in a law firm and £16,000 a year and covering childcare and expenses and working with people and when you 'see' yourself in an interview, confident like your brother that's confident ... like what?

M: Like ... like the large teddy on my little boy's bed that my brother gave him for his birthday. (smiles) Yes that's it. The bear looks confident and a bit like my brother with his red cap on the side of his head.

C: And large teddy, looks confident like your brother and you 'see' yourself at interview and is there anything else about confident like that?

M: It's a nice picture and makes me laugh.

C: And when nice picture and see yourself at interview and confident like the large teddy, what happens to tight feeling in your stomach?

M: The tightness eases, and it feels more relaxed.

C: And when eases and more relaxed and see yourself at interview and law firm and £16,000 a year for child care and expenses, then what happens?

M: Then I can look for a job with a better feeling about myself and it doesn't feel so daunting. I can think about the picture of a confident large teddy and remind myself of my brother and how he always manages to stay positive. I think I can draw strength from that.

C: *Is there anything else about a job working with others and you need money? (her original outcome)*

M: Yes I need to start looking for a job today.

In this session Mandy developed an anchor (the confident large teddy) to access as a reference point for when she was feeling tight in her stomach. Until then she had had a negative feeling about 'fluffing' the interview (we found another anchor for the 'fluff' in a subsequent session – it became the soft fur of the large bear that she could stroke to make her feel calm).

Mandy was then able to start looking for a job with a more positive mindset. She began to mentally rehearse how she would be in the interview (confident and calm). We explored some challenging situations she might face and how she could stay focused on her experience, skills and qualities. Three months later she managed to go to her first interview with a law firm in the City. She visualized the large teddy sitting in the room beside her giving her support and encouragement. She was delighted when she was offered the job at £18,000 a year.

Putting aside your negative associations and replacing them with more positive 'anchors' can really free up your mind. They act as a signal that allows you to focus on what you are capable of and increases motivation.

Case study

Nick had watched his brother drown in a neighbour's swimming pool when he was ten years old. His brother was two years younger and he had not been able to save him. He had carried this guilt around for years and it had really stopped him from finding a job where he was happy and fulfilled (Nick's desired outcome). Over several sessions he was able to 'wrap his guilt in a soft blanket' and 'carry his brother gently inside it' in this way he was able to 'take care of' his brother and allow himself to move forward more positively. This was a powerful anchor and enabled him to be the successful and fulfilled maths teacher he had always wanted to be.

Creating rapport and using NLP for discussions and problem solving

When taking part in any assessment, group presentation or discussion there are useful NLP strategies that can be applied.

One NLP tip is to listen to your preferred speaking style (VAK) and those of others. For example, if you are visual it is possible you will use more 'seeing' words than someone who is auditory and uses more 'hearing' words. However, this is not an exact practice as much of the language we use is copied from our environment. Having said this, when problem solving, questions such as 'What do you think?', 'Do you want to accept this?' or 'Does this seem Ok?' can promote restrictive one-word responses and are often not helpful in discussions. If you shift to questions that appeal to the senses, such as 'How do you *feel* about...?', 'What solutions do you *see* here?' or 'That *sounds* possible doesn't it?' you tend to get more expansive and creative responses. These questions are generally more appealing and it becomes easier to create rapport in discussions.

Other NLP methods helpful in discussions and problem solving are:

PACING AND LEADING

When pacing you use subtle mirroring techniques to match the tone, volume, speed and stress patterns used by your interviewer or colleagues. This also extends to the body language, posture and gestures which can instantly strengthen relationships.

If you observe people who are in a close relationship or who work together frequently, they unconsciously mirror each other in this way. When you first begin to practise this you will find it is often automatic and natural. In no way should this be overt and clumsy as this can be patronizing and offensive. Done well this is a soft and authentic way of building relationships and creating rapport. It does however need practice and skill to be truly effective.

Leading in a discussion or problem-solving task can be another subtle way to make your point clearly, reduce conflict or bring a heated discussion to a more manageable level. This is done by matching the body language, preferred style, voice tone, and volume of the group at the start and then gradually reducing the speed, and volume to a calmer level. At the same time use solution-focused, in this case, visual words that match your colleague, such as 'Yes, I quite *see* that can be the case [strong tone and volume]. However, perhaps another way of *looking* at this could be ... [slowing the pace and reducing the volume]'.

Case study

A client of mine, Jake, works with a volatile line manager and asked me if I had any strategies he could use to cope with this. Often the line manager is stressed. He tends to deal with issues at full volume and can be very dogmatic. Jake told me he had tried staying calm but this seemed to exacerbate the problem. I asked him to imagine a time when he had been angry or frustrated and if he would respond well to someone who was calm and in control. He soon realized that, actually, no – he wouldn't!

Jake worked on some firm yet positive responses he could use and how he could initially match the volume and voice tone of his line manager. He focused on specific solution-focused language. In addition, he gradually slowed his pace and lowered the volume after the initial matching, and this reduced the tension considerably. He found that his line manager responded well after the first outburst and it increased the understanding between them.

Conversely, if someone is sad or feeling low it is also unhelpful to exclaim what a wonderful day it is or how nice they look in an effort to cheer them up! What is most helpful is to match their feeling initially and then gradually bring them to a more positive place. The same is true if you have a colleague in a group who is reluctant to give an opinion. Asking quietly if they would like to contribute and then creating space and listening will often bring a response that was previously not forthcoming. This is using the NLP techniques of matching, pacing and leading with care and with a genuine wish to build relationships.

Focus points

The main points to remember from this chapter are:

* Mental preparation is key.
* Mental rehearsal can be used to banish negative thoughts.
* Anchors can help to overcome negative past experiences.
* Pacing and leading can be used to create rapport.
* There are a variety of NLP techniques that can help you at interview.

Next step

In the next chapter you will look at the more advanced competency based interviews. You will discover what 'laddering' questions are and how to prepare for them. You will also find out about assessment centres, and how psychometric and personality testing is carried out.

Assessments

In this chapter you will discover:

▶ *How to approach competency-based interviews*

▶ *How to tackle psychometric and personality testing*

▶ *What to expect from assessment centres*

Competency-based interviews

If you are invited for a competency-based interview you will need time to prepare and develop specific examples of where you have performed well.

This is the time to really sell your own skills (what you can do) and behaviours (how you do them) and to demonstrate knowledge and expertise. Do not be put off if you have been out of work for a while as you can draw on your hobbies and leisure activities for examples.

Competency means showing the appropriate level of ability to handle tasks, problems, projects and so on, effectively. It also means demonstrating appropriate behaviours, such as being on time, reliable and committed to the role. The interviewer will have drawn up a list of acceptable criteria and behaviours you will be measured against. This is where you need to really dig deep and explore your strengths and positive behavioural traits.

Think back to situations where you have performed well and really achieved positive results. Examples from your personal life could be:

▶ how you joined a sports club and won a prize at a competitive event

▶ the way in which you have managed your household single-handed

▶ how you have volunteered and worked for a community project.

Some of the skills and behaviours show determination to succeed, working with others, good organizational skills, ability to multi-task, staying focused on your goal, motivating others, etc.

Try it now: Past performance

Find your own examples by looking back over your life and visualizing those times when you really performed well. Take your time over this and stay focused on your desired outcome – your new job.

If you are experienced and have some examples of work-related skills and behaviours, then one suggestion is to use the computer or take a large piece of paper and coloured pens. Draw a line down the centre and on one side write 'Skills/Knowledge' and on the other 'Behaviours/Qualities'. Then go back over your recent jobs and decide on several specific examples that could demonstrate your skills and positive behaviours.

You will need four or five examples that might cover aspects of your intended job role showing a variety of skills and behaviours:

✻ What you did (skills, knowledge)
✻ How you did it (behaviours and actions)
✻ What the results were (outcomes)
✻ What you learnt (improvements for next time)

At this stage just note down everything you can think of, even if they are not role specific. They will be useful in jogging your memory for other areas of work you may not have thought of.

If it appeals to you, it may be helpful to develop a metaphor for when you are working at your best. Look over what you have written and notice the skills and behaviours you have identified as your strengths.

If we take a Clean Language question we would ask:

> So when you are working in this way and at your best you are like ... what?

Here's a few examples I have taken from clients' responses to this question:

> **Julia:** I'm someone who pays attention to detail and enjoys project work, so when I'm working at my best I think I'm like a portrait painter. They have the person in front of them so they know exactly what the project is. They can decide how to paint the portrait and what colours to use where. They also need to pay attention to detail, get the likeness and reflect the qualities of the person.

Another response was:

> **Andrea:** Well, I really love leading a team and collaborating with others. I have good people skills and I have been told I have a high level of emotional intelligence. So when I'm working at my best, a metaphor I could use would be that of a matriarch in a herd of horses. She leads but is very sensitive to others in the herd and nurtures those who are younger and less experienced. She watches out for danger and keeps them safe.

Often developing a metaphor will stay with you and enable you to focus more easily on your key abilities and strengths. Take a moment to ask yourself:

> When I'm working at my best, I'm like ... what?

When you have identified specific areas of work that really show your skills and behaviours in a positive light, it is time to look at the kind of questions you may be asked by the interviewer or assessor.

LADDERING QUESTIONS

In competency-based interviews a technique called 'laddering' is often used. This technique allows the interviewer to delve down into the reasons for your actions and uncover your core values. They tend to develop and dig deeper into the areas you have identified. Let's look at some examples.

One question at the beginning of the interview could be:

> Can you explain a situation where you have worked on your own initiative?

The laddering questions may be:

▶ What specific skills/qualities did you need for this situation?

▶ How did you manage to motivate yourself?

▶ If things had not gone as you would have liked, what would you have done?

▶ Why is it important for people to use their own initiative, in your opinion?

A further example:

> Can you explain a situation where you had to motivate others?

Then the laddering questions could be posed as follows:

▶ What specifically did you do to motivate them?

▶ What actions did you take to ensure they stayed on track?

- What worked well and not so well in this situation?

- What did you learn from this?

A further example might be:

> Please outline a time when you were able to meet your deadlines for a project.

Then the laddering questions may be:

- How did you plan in order to meet those deadlines?

- What skills and qualities were important for you and your team to demonstrate?

- If you were to pick one skill and one behaviour that were key to the success of this project, what would they be?

- Would you do anything differently when faced with a similar situation again?

Another example could be:

> Can you relate a situation where you were able to communicate a difficult or challenging message to your staff?

The laddering questions may be:

- How did you manage to allay their reservations/fears?

- What enabled you to deliver this message effectively?

- What impact did this have on your staff/on you?

- If faced with a similar situation, would you do the same again or change anything?

Once you have an idea of how the laddering questions work it is easy to apply them to your own examples. Preparing in this way can really set you apart from the other interviewees and give you the edge.

Notice the way the final two questions are formed in order for you to say what you learnt. Do not focus on what went wrong or any mistakes you made. Merely say briefly what you learnt and focus on the positive steps you would take next time.

Open questions work best, particularly 'what?', 'which?' and 'how?', and then 'if...?' questions to test possible scenarios.

All interviews need the three 'Ps': planning, preparation and practice. With this in mind, competency-based interviews are a ready-made situation for positive mental rehearsal to see you through. Top sports people and frequent public speakers would not dream of going to an event without mental rehearsal. By applying some simple NLP strategies (such as those in the case studies in Chapter 6) before your interview you can really be at your best.

Psychometric and personality testing

As part of your interview you might come across psychometric tests, which are structured methods used by employers to assess each candidate's suitability for a job. They may include aptitude or ability tests, personality questionnaires or a combination of both. Psychometric testing is usually one part of a multi-stage recruitment process as you will see from the section on assessment centres below. Sometimes you may be requested to do aptitude tests online within a set time period before you are asked for interview. If so, approach them with a positive mindset and be prepared to learn from the process. There are often no right or wrong answers, just those more appropriate to the role or position in the company. Try to answer as truthfully as possible. There is no point in trying to 'fit' what you feel is appropriate, you'll soon be found out! Remember you want to be taken on because of your own unique personality, knowledge and skill set.

I was running a team away day for the staff of an IT company. Members of the four teams (A, B, C, D) were given a task to complete, while at the same time competing against the other teams. This involved reading instructions in order to finish the task effectively and win. At the bottom of the page in small print was written the following: 'If you collaborate with another team you will finish this task quicker and more effectively.' Only one team, 'B', noticed this and quietly informed their colleagues in team 'A'; they won over teams C and D, who had neglected to notice the small print!

Take your time and read all the instructions!

Below are a few of the most common tests and questionnaires so that you can familiarize yourself with the terms used.

Personality profiling: These are usually multiple-choice questions with a simple tick response. They are not testing you on anything specific, merely trying to see how your personality fits with the organization.

Numerical and verbal reasoning: You will be presented with simple calculations or asked to identify patterns, sequences, graphs and so on. For verbal reasoning you will be given language-based tests and you may be asked to process and analyse a variety of texts or scripts. For a particular role you may also be tested on spelling, grammar and syntax.

IQ tests: These are becoming rarer (and usually test your spatial and diagrammatical reasoning and awareness) and being replaced with emotional and social intelligence tests.

Emotional and social intelligence tests: These can be a selection of problems, issues or work situations that frequently arise. You are asked to briefly describe how you would address the issue and find a suitable approach or solution.

Mechanical/technical aptitude: These tests will assess your practical ability in whatever field you are working. Keep in mind that all tests will give you valuable experience and treat them as an aid to learning more about the role.

Remember this

You will not always be asked to find a solution, merely to show you can think on your feet, respond appropriately, and possibly take some action.

An example could be, a member of staff comes to you to complain that they are being bullied by their line manager. How would you tackle this situation?

Or, the team you are managing appears demotivated and is not engaging well with the current project. What action would you take to address this?

Even if you can only come up with a couple of suggestions, that will be sufficient.

Assessment centres

When going for interview you will find that some organizations use assessment centres in their recruitment process. These generally last one or two days and are held after the first round of interviews and before the final selection.

Often they can also be used as an initial selection process. You will be asked to participate in a number of activities and exercises during which assessors will observe and rate your performance. If you approach this with an interested and positive mindset then it can be a very useful experience. This is a chance to interact with other interviewees and to take part in exercises where you will learn and increase you knowledge.

In my book *Coaching Skills for Leaders in the Workplace*, I suggest self-supervision questions to ask yourself as a leader/coach. These are questions such as: 'What needs to happen for me to be better organized, punctual, complete projects, not get anxious, etc?' or 'What one action can I take that would help me to start this report/presentation/task?' Self-assessment questions can form the basis of your preparation for the assessment centre and need close attention.

Make sure you are calm with no interruptions and able to take time to reflect on the following questions. Some have been answered for you in previous chapters.

Questions you can ask yourself:

✳ What do I need to do, think about or change to believe in myself?
✳ Have I read the job description thoroughly and matched my skills appropriately?
✳ Have I visited the website and read about the company and made notes?
✳ How can I gain a greater insight into what is expected of me?
✳ What do I expect from myself during this assessment?
✳ Have I made a note of my own strengths, skills and key behaviours?
✳ What affirmations can I write for myself?
✳ Can I give concrete examples to show my skills and abilities?
✳ If I need to give a presentation have I prepared and practised it?
✳ What can I do to remain calm and in control?
✳ What visualizations or other NLP techniques can I apply?
✳ What questions do I want to ask the interviewers?
✳ What questions do I want to ask my fellow interviewees?

You may encounter the following at assessment centres:

Informal gatherings: These are where you can meet a variety of people, including other candidates, the assessors, and the management team. You need to take into account that you are being assessed from the minute you walk into the room. Stand tall with your shoulders back and walk in with confidence – even if you don't feel it! Approach a group, smile and introduce yourself. Be friendly but take time to listen to others and be curious. There may also be further information given during this session about the company and the various jobs on offer. Listen out for any information that is new or relevant to your intended role.

Assessment tests: These are specifically designed and can be used to reveal, for example, your personality type, how well you perform in a team and to test your potential. There are many of these tests online and you can practise them beforehand. MBTI, DISC, BELBIN, HONEY and MUMFORD are just some that are available. Assessors may also measure you against a set of previously prepared competencies. Each exercise is designed to assess different aspects and areas of performance.

Again, use this as an opportunity to learn and grow. You will not perform at your best if you are worried about the results. You can only do your best and you can refer to your metaphor from previously to anchor you during this process. Ask yourself 'When I am doing this assessment the best I can, I'm like ... what?' Find a positive image or metaphor as you did before. You can choose what to believe and what to think about during this process. If you are calm and willing to learn you will gain a lot. Sometimes the journey can be as rewarding as the goal. Treat each interview and assessment as a learning curve and build on your knowledge. Your confidence will grow and each time you will do a little better.

A TYPICAL ASSESSMENT DAY

You have done your research via the organization's website.

You made a list of your main strengths and relevant skills and behaviours.

Your list of self-assessment questions have been completed.

You have arrived in time and dressed smartly.

While mingling with other candidates, you have picked up further information.

The next stage is the individual interviews and assessment tests.

After that you will be given several exercises to discuss and problems to solve, often with other candidates. These will be based on the kind of work you have applied for. Be sure to listen carefully to the instructions. Breathe and notice what is going on around you – it is often at this stage where candidates miss vital information key to the tasks.

These tasks vary but could be one or more of the following:

A group presentation topic: This is usually given to a group of two to four people who jointly discuss the key points and decide on who will present which elements. This tests your communication skills in the group, during the presentation and also shows your ability to organize key points and work as a team.

A panel discussion: This involves three or four people who usually have a problem or issue to solve between them. This is always connected to the job role you will be applying for. Your listening, decision-making and negotiation skills will be assessed in this task.

An in-tray task: This requires you to assume a particular role as an employee and work through the tasks in your in-tray. Skills assessed are generally your ability to organize data and prioritize work.

A problem-solving exercise: This can be given to an individual or small group. A problem is discussed and a solution to suit all parties arrived at. This tests your analytical skills, your ability to listen and persuade and tests your problem solving skills.

A case study (group): This is usually given to a small group for discussion and analysis. This is often a real situation that has occurred in the organization. Your leadership, influencing and creative thinking skills are tested along with your ability to build trust and rapport with your team members.

A case study (individual): This can be more of a challenge as you will be presented with background documentation and pre-set questions. Then you will have a period of time to consider them and to prepare your response. This tests your ability to reason, problem solve and think laterally.

Here are some tips to bear in mind:

► Listen really well as you are given the task.

► Take time to read and absorb the documents.

► Control your breathing and stay calm and in control.

► Cut out any 'chatter' that is unhelpful.

► Go through the questions and highlight the key words/phrases.

► Break the problem down.

► Select key elements for consideration and analysis.

► Test your reasoning and assumptions.

► Reach your conclusion.

At this stage the assessment will focus more on your behaviour, your reasoning and ability to think on your feet. Later the focus is on your interaction with the other candidates. Your assessors are there to make you feel at ease and to show your strengths. This is not so much about what you know, more about you as an individual, your thought processes and, when in group activities, your ability as a team player/leader.

A further selection of the kind of skills and abilities you will be assessed on are:

- building relationships
- creating rapport with others
- building trust
- working as a team
- strengths as an individual
- taking initiative
- how you communicate
- influencing
- leadership
- showing integrity
- listening and attention to detail
- staying focused and on task
- data analysis
- time management
- motivation and positive mindset
- decision-making
- creativity and original thinking.

For further preparation you might go through the above and ask yourself where your strengths lie and where you need to improve. What behaviours do you need to focus on in order to improve? This is best done with a colleague or friend who can give you honest feedback!

On the assessment day, focus on your strengths and qualities. You may find out that you have hidden talents or strengths you had not realized. Stay natural and true to yourself. Above all, listen well and enjoy the day as far as possible.

Focus points

The main points to remember from this chapter are:

* Prepare well for competency-based interviews.
* Approach assessments with a positive mindset.
* Stay calm and willing to learn during any assessment.

Next step

In part three you will be thinking about strategies to put in place after the interview. You will consider the possible pitfalls of being too positive or too confident. You will look at ways to handle rejection and still move forward in your quest. If you got the job then how do you negotiate the best deal for yourself and put your views across firmly?

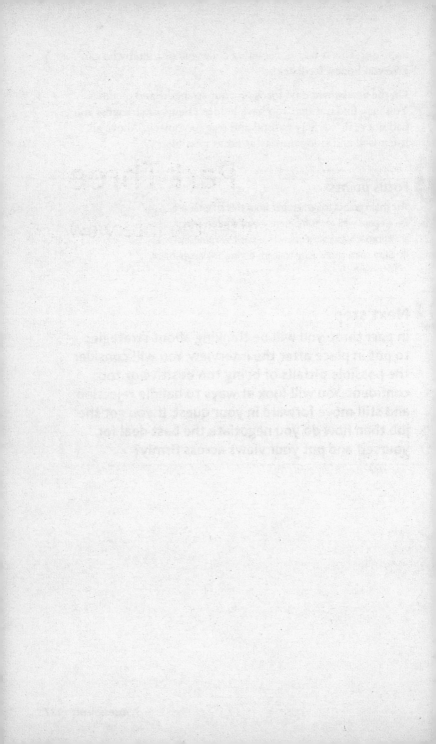

Part Three

After the Interview

Dealing with What Happens Next

In this chapter you will discover:

▶ *Can you be too positive?*
▶ *How to handle rejection*
▶ *How to keep calm and model success*
▶ *What happens when you get the job*

Once you have had the interview and you are waiting for the results, you need to re-energize yourself to start your search again. This means returning to the first chapter and taking yourself back on the journey.

Being too positive

There are times when one job seems to stand out as the one for you. At times like this it can be easy to put all your focus on this one job and discard other vacancies. You can never be absolutely sure that one job is better than another. Even if a job seems to really fit your qualifications and experience, there may, for example, be no opportunities for promotion. If you pin all your hopes on one job then you can often be disappointed. The balance between being positive and over-confident is a fine one as we see below.

Case study

Amy was looking for a job as a PA and she saw an advert online that really sparked her interest. She decided to apply for this job and we worked together on the techniques you have experienced in this book. She became very excited about this position as it involved setting up conferences and events which she really enjoyed. She became convinced that this was the job for her and began to focus all her energies on this *one* job. When she was asked back for a second interview she was thrilled.

We discussed in her coaching sessions how important it was for her to spread her energy over several jobs and not place her hopes on any particular one. However, Amy was convinced she would get this position and therefore she gave up looking for other positions during this time. This was her own choice and despite our coaching sessions and warnings from her own family she was simply blind to other offers she had received.

Naturally she was devastated when another candidate was given the position. When they called she asked them what she could have done better or differently. The feedback was that her knowledge of setting up events was not as extensive as the successful candidate.

Amy took several weeks to come to terms with what had happened. She slowly realized that pinning all her hopes on one job was not practical and that there were several jobs that matched her skills and experience. Amy found another two jobs that suited her skills and experience and she prepared for them both over the following weeks. She also kept looking, both online and by contacting colleagues on internet networking sites. After three months Amy was successful and is now working as a PA in an events company. The job is not local as she would have liked (she has to commute for 40 minutes) but she feels that the experience will be useful for her in future. The main thing is that she loves the job and has plenty of opportunities for promotion. These were two of her original values and aims.

Sometimes being too positive and losing focus can be counter-productive. There needs to be a measured approach and placing your hopes on one job is certainly not the way to go. As far as possible, select at least three that you can focus on at any one time. Continue your search, even when you have received an interview or feel you have done well. This way you will avoid disappointment and have something to fall back on should your interview not be successful.

What happens when you don't get any of the jobs you applied for?

How to handle rejection

If you have been for several interviews and have applied for at least five jobs without success then it is time to re-assess. Even if you have retrained, are up to date with your skills and have some experience of the roles you are applying for, rejection is a part of the process. This can happen for a number of reasons not necessarily due to your lack of knowledge or skills. Nearly everyone I have worked with has been turned down at some point in their job search. This is not personal, just the way the process works. At this point it is vital to stay focused and take stock of what has happened. You have invested time and energy in applying for and researching the company and this has not been wasted. All knowledge and experience is useful, you may not realize this right now but it will most likely serve you in the future.

Remember this

If you have been turned down several times, you will naturally be feeling low. The best way to solve this is to take exercise. Choose something you like, even if it's only running up and down the stairs at home, jogging in the park or dancing to music. Any form of exercise is a real motivator and will help to release your feelings of frustration.

Case study

Jake was feeling really unhappy after a job interview had, in his view, not gone well. He had taken the rejection really personally. He had not realized the job had been given to someone who had already been with the company for two years. When he wrote to the company for feedback he realized it was just bad luck. They had recruited internally and there was nothing more he could have done. Nonetheless, Jake was feeling down and lacking in motivation until he thought of taking up cycling again.

He had given up his car a couple of months previously as he couldn't afford to continue to run it. Now he was taking public transport and he made the decision to 'get on his bike'. He reported that this significantly changed his life as he felt much fitter and more motivated. Happily as a result of taking part in a fun run during the summer he chanced to meet his future employer.

This just proves that you can find employment in surprising places! Naturally Jake was delighted when, after a panel interview, this new contact offered him a job with his firm.

Some of the following thoughts and questions may help ease your sense of frustration.

▶ You did your best and this job was just not for you this time.

▶ Everyone can gain useful insights from being turned down.

▶ Every interview will give you experience and increase your knowledge.

▶ Every interview gives you the best practice possible!

▶ Do you know why you were not successful – did you ask?

- Feedback is useful for your future interviews so asking what you could have done better/differently is more power to you!

- You were not turned down on a personal level – it was the job role that you were not successful in achieving. There is a big difference.

- Most recruiters will be looking for more people in the future so write a brief thank you note (about a week after the interview is best).

- Sometimes the job is not accepted by the successful applicant.

- Other positions may become available in this or a sister company.

- Your job search carries on regardless.

- The right job often eventually appears when you least expect it. Will you be ready?

It is never a good idea to assume you have got the job or to assume you haven't! What you need to do is to continue to search for your ideal job in exactly the same way as you did before your first interview. Why? Take a look at this list and then you will realize how important it is to stay focused on your job search.

Consider:

- What if you don't get this job? How will you feel if you base all your hopes on this one?

- What if you do a trial period and find that the job is not what you expected?

- What if they ask you to leave after the trial period is up?

- What if your life changes and you can no longer work in this job/at this location?

All of the above can happen and so staying on track is essential. In ever changing markets you cannot afford to be complacent.

Bearing this in mind it is a useful idea to write to your prospective employer after your interview to thank them for their time. Of course, after your interview you will have a very clear idea of what they are looking for and the way your own skills and knowledge can be of benefit to them. This letter is also a good opportunity to remind them very briefly of how you can match their requirements. Receiving a letter from a potential candidate at this stage is unusual and you will immediately impress them as someone who pays attention to detail and follows up on actions. The letter needs to be very brief, addressed to the main interviewer covering the key points only and sent the day after the interview – later and the impact will be lost or it will be overlooked.

Not all companies take the time to respond to candidates who have not been successful. This is even more reason to keep on track with your job search. Nonetheless, it is useful for you to know the result, so if you have not heard anything after ten days, call them to enquire if they have made a decision. If you were not successful, ask them if they are willing to give you feedback as this can really be a great help for further interviews. You may not want to hear what they say but at least you will gain useful information to take forward. Don't be afraid to ask!

You weren't successful – now what?

There are a number of strategies and tips that you can use if you are not proving to be successful at interview.

First go back to the beginning of the book and make sure you are following the NLP strategies and self-coaching techniques outlined. (Clear outcome, clarity around your skills and knowledge, good preparation and knowledge of the company, positive mindset, mental preparation, visualization, breathing, calm place and so on.)

Then if possible set up a mock interview with a couple of colleagues or friends who will give you honest and constructive feedback. If you do not have anyone you feel comfortable with, hire a career coach to support you.

One very good way to see where you might be going wrong is to video the interview. There is really no substitute for watching yourself on film and noticing your behaviour, body language, speech patterns and questioning techniques first hand!

Case study

Geoff had gone for several interviews before he contacted me. He had been out of work for seven months and was very despondent. I suggested we set up a video interview so that I could give him some constructive feedback. He agreed, although he was very reluctant at first!

In his previous role he had been a security guard at a construction company, where he was made redundant. He was looking for a similar role this time. When he watched the interview back he was really surprised to notice that he was leaning right forward with his elbows on the interviewer's table. In Geoff's words, 'I'm right in his face, aren't I?' Also after some gentle questioning he picked up that he was quite aggressive in his tone when answering the interviewer's questions.

I introduced Geoff to perceptual positions and asked him to sit in the 'interviewer's chair' and then be 'an observer' of both himself and the interviewer. The result was a real breakthrough as Geoff noticed several areas where he had not responded appropriately. These insights were slowly addressed and we did three more videoed interviews over the next two months. Geoff managed to secure a position as a security guard for an automobile company four months later.

Sometimes you may be unaware of what is holding you back from securing a position. It may be those habits and patterns of behaviour that have become old friends and are difficult to shift, despite your efforts to put them aside. This next technique might be just what you are looking for!

Modelling success

NLP has its roots in finding out what makes people successful. So what exactly is modelling and how can it help you to success at interview? Modelling means replicating and understanding what it is that enables some people to be more successful than others. By breaking down what someone does into easy stages you can create a model (role model) for yourself. Let me give you an example.

The television programme *Dragons' Den* gives aspiring business people the opportunity to be 'interviewed' in front of a panel. The business men and women then get the chance to have one or two highly successful entrepreneurs work with them on their business. Members of the public who have started a business present their business case and ask the entrepreneurs to invest large amounts of money so they can succeed with their products and services in the marketplace.

This programme has broken down the process so that any member of the public with a business idea has a chance to be 'interviewed' by the panel. As the programme has gone on, it has demonstrated that those that have modelled previous successful candidates usually win the support they ask for. Those aspiring business owners have successfully broken the stages down into:

▶ good personal image and presentation skills

▶ high level of passion and enthusiasm

▶ excellent knowledge of the business model and company background

▶ in-depth understanding of the financial aspects of the business

▶ ability to 'field' questions and ask intelligent questions of the panel.

These business people have modelled themselves on the skills and knowledge of past successful candidates. As a result, they have secured a sound investment and the support of a highly successful entrepreneur.

This does not mean these start-up business people are copying others, as they will not have the same business or the same skills and abilities. However, they have identified the key elements (behaviours, attitude, process) that make for a successful interview and presentation. You can do this too by watching this programme and others like it. Another way is by observing others being interviewed on the internet and learning from them.

When you go for an interview it is useful for you to model someone you know who has been successful and got that job! See if you can set up an interview with them to find out what they did and thought and what skills you would like to model.

In the course of my work I do a number of conference workshops and presentations. I practise and prepare for these events and part of this preparation is to watch highly motivational speakers online. The skills and techniques I have modelled greatly enhance my delivery and every time I watch someone I learn a great deal.

Here are some questions to ask using all the senses when you are 'modelling someone' (or looking for a 'role model') who has been successful at interview or giving presentations.

▶ What key *actions and thoughts* motivated you in the weeks before your interview?

▶ How did you overcome your *feelings* of nervousness?

▶ What *actions* did you take that day, before you left?

▶ What specifically did you *think about* on the way to the interview?

▶ What did you *visualize* before you started?

Remember this

When asking these questions, some thoughts and actions can be unconscious and people may not be aware of what they do. As soon as you get a response, help the person to remember by using laddering questions.

Case study

Katie was modelling her colleague who had just secured a really good position, she taped her interview with him and this is the tape script (names have been changed to ensure confidentiality).

(K: Katie, J: John)

K: John, what did you think about in the run up to the interview that helped you?

J: Umm, not sure really, I just tried to stay focused on a positive outcome.

(Katie took John's words – 'positive outcome' and asked more about that with a 'clean' question.)

K: So you thought about a positive outcome, what kind of positive outcome was that?

J: Well, that I would be able to answer their questions and that the job I was applying for was really interesting. I tried to look forward to the interview as a useful experience.

(So now Katie had quite a bit more information to work with and ask further questions – notice how she **laddered** the questions using 'useful experience'.)

K: Yes, you mentioned you looked forward to the interview as a useful experience, is there anything else about 'useful experience' in this context?

J: Umm, I suppose I was not too attached to the outcome of the interview. I was interested in *experiencing* the way the company worked and getting to know the people.

K: What did you pay attention to while you were experiencing how the company worked?

J: Wow, that's quite hard to say! In the first panel interview I had three interviewers. I really listened to how they described their roles and the way they outlined what the company is hoping to achieve. So listening carefully for information, staying interested in what they had to say and noticing the interaction between them. Somehow I didn't really notice this at the time, but now you ask I think that's what I did.

K: So you were listening, being interested and noticing the interaction between them. Were the questions they asked also part of your focus on having a 'useful experience'?

J: Yes, definitely. The questions in a panel interview are often quite challenging and I needed to tell myself that all the questions would add to my experience and knowledge, no matter what the outcome.

K: So in your mind the interview was just adding to your knowledge and experience. When the questions are challenging, what actions or thoughts did you rehearse in order to stay calm?

(Katie now asks about the *questions* as a new line of enquiry.)

J: Well, I'm quite visual so as part of my preparation I sketched the panel of interviewers and dressed them in prisoner's uniforms! As you know I'm applying for a job as a barrister so this seemed to be quite appropriate. It really helped me to view them as non-threatening and then their *questions* didn't seem so challenging either.

K: That's a great visual and I can see how that helped you. And is there anything else about the way you viewed the challenging questions?

J: Let's see, I typed them all on the computer and used different colours for the different types of *questions*. That worked well and helped as a memory aid too.

K: How did using different colours for the questions work well for you?

J: I could categorize the kind of questions I thought they might ask so they were clear in my mind. This kept me focused on the process and content of the interview. This also meant that I didn't jump all over the place with my own questions and that worked well. Having the colours in my mind also made me feel more relaxed.

(Katie was now interested in modelling how John became more relaxed so she asked another 'clean' question.)

K: And having the colours made you more focused on the process and content and feel more relaxed. And what happens just before you feel relaxed like that?

J: Well, if I have a colourful visual it always takes me to a relaxing place in my mind. It's as if I am in my studio painting a picture and it seems to take the sting out of any situation.

K: So it seems as if a colourful visual really helps to relax you. And is there anything else about feeling more relaxed that helps?

J: Yes, doing some gentle exercise and breathing deeply before the interview helps me to relax too. I used a combination of breathing and visualization both before the panel interview and when I had to do the ten minute presentation.

In this interview with John, it becomes clear that there are thoughts, actions, visualizations, feelings and strategies for a successful interview that Katie can model for herself. Naturally she will adopt the kind of sense stimulus that works best for her. Added to which, knowing the way John was thinking and acting really helped her to look at things differently.

This is a story I overheard that illustrates what I mean.

Two couples had recently moved into a new estate at the base of some lovely mountains in the highlands of Scotland. They were neighbours and often chatted over the fence. One day the two men decided to take a hike up the nearest mountain. When they were almost at the top they spotted a beautiful stag standing majestically on the ridge.

First man: 'Oh what a beautiful sight I wish I had my camera.'

Second man: 'Yes he's a great specimen, how I wish I had bought my gun!'

Neither of the two men was wrong to think the way they did – it was just that they had different views of the situation according to their upbringing. They thought about and viewed the experience in different ways and through different filters.

Each person is unique and memories and ideas are formed as a result of where you live, how you were educated, who your parents were and the influences of those around you. This causes you to have preferences and make decisions that may be different from others.

In NLP this is called filtering and is a way everyone pays attention to what is going on in the world. In this age of vast knowledge and advanced technology, everything is so fast paced that it is impossible to capture all the stimuli you receive on a daily basis. So you have developed the ability to delete and sometimes distort the information you receive. You focus your attention on those things that are important to you and don't notice others.

Perhaps while you have been reading you have noticed that you enjoy some parts of the book more than others. You may feel like doing some exercises and techniques more than others. Do you listen to music while reading or have the computer running? Do you notice the trees moving outside or traffic noise or sounds from the street in the background? Some of these experiences may have been out of your awareness and were being filtered without you being aware of it.

The same is true of your daily conversations and the information exchange in interviews. How much of the last interview between Katie and John do you remember? Did you notice specifically what had helped John before and during the interview – what exactly stayed in your mind and what did you filter?

An example Katie reported to me at the end of her conversation with John is that she needed to ask him to really drill down as she found him quite vague in his responses. This is because John has a 'big picture' and more general way of expressing himself and this was quite frustrating for Katie who wanted specific details. For example, John said 'I used different colours for the different types of *questions*. That worked well.'

What Katie needed to know was how using colours worked well, and what 'well' meant. If Katie was to distort John words she would be bringing in her own interpretation of what he said using her own experience. This is akin to mind reading, which can often be completely inaccurate and is to be avoided.

Obviously in an interview situation when you are asked a question in a certain way, it is essential to notice what you are filtering, to clarify meaning and to avoid distortions! Just because one of your interview panel is looking stern or seems abrupt may not mean he dislikes you (your interpretation/distortion). He may just be having a bad day or has had a row with a family member.

The strategies and techniques in this book have outlined some of the ways in which you can coach yourself to your desired outcome and model success. This takes time and determination, and as several skills and techniques are involved you will need focus and motivation.

Remember this

Thinking about your interview, it is useful to consider that you are offering the company the opportunity to employ you, rather than they have a job to offer. Your attitude is key!

If you held the empowering beliefs you have worked on throughout this book, how would you be acting and thinking? What would you be saying, feeling? Remember to do the exercises day in, day out, so that they become regular confident habits.

Enhancing your commitment

Throughout this book you have read about the power of creating metaphors and you were encouraged to think 'when you're at your best facing the interview panel, you're like ... what?' Perhaps you came up with a powerful metaphor as some of the people in the case studies did. I hope so, as this will really support your commitment to finding a good job.

Try it now: Clean questions about your metaphor

If you have your metaphor and you have drawn it (if not, this is the time to get it on paper or designed on the computer), try asking some 'clean' questions around your metaphor. These kinds of questions are designed to get you to access unconscious thoughts and build your metaphors so that they can support you in times of stress and uncertainty. You should use these questions by inserting your own language into the question and building on your visual. If you can find a colleague or friend to do this exercise with, then all the better as you will be able to help each other.

As a coach I use the metaphor of an eagle that hovers above my clients, allowing them to find their own answers and take responsibility for their actions. I see myself high up in the distance and ready to swoop down to support if necessary.

So the clean elements of questions (in bold) I use to gain even more clarity are:

▶ **And what kind of** eagle is that when it's above your clients?

▶ And **is there anything else about** an eagle like that?

- **And where is** that eagle that hovers above?

- **And what size and shape** is that eagle? (Or if you do not have something tangible then ask: And **does it have a size or a shape?**)

- **And is there a relationship between** 'distance and 'support?'

- **And what happens** just before swoop down?

- **And when you swoop down** to support, **then what happens?**

Once you have asked these questions you will have further insights into your metaphorical landscape and the meaning will be clearer. You may want to add to your drawing and enhance the picture.

Now ask yourself what is the most important element of your metaphor. Whatever is the most important word or phrase in your metaphor, extract it and build it into your picture or visual representation. Now you should have a really powerful and developed metaphor to take forward.

You got the job – excellent news!

So you got the job and your first day is looming. How do you prepare?

Look through the contract carefully and check out the following:

(*Note that not all these will apply to every job, this is just an overview.*)

- your job role and responsibilities

- who you report to – check out who will be your boss

- your hours of work

- holiday pay, sick pay and bonus system

- pension plans and any contributions

- travelling expenses

- commission paid or profit share

- if there is a staff canteen

- staff discounts

- transport possibilities to and from work

- car allowance or company car

- what training and support is offered, if any

- what their policy is on Health and Safety (if applicable)

- their terms and conditions

- childcare or nursery

- notice period when terminating the contract (both sides).

Take time to read through your contract with a fine tooth comb and then you will be in a position to negotiate any areas you are not happy with. If you are starting at a low salary, take a look at the additional benefits as they may add up to quite a bit.

Case study

Mike had been offered a position in a company quite far from his home and had decided that the salary he was offered was too low. After reading the contract carefully with him, I pointed out that with the generous travel allowance, company car and staff canteen he could add on another £3,000 a year. Naturally, the commute was a factor but on balance he decided to accept the offer as it was a job he really enjoyed.

This is the reason why it is so important to check the details of your contract.

If you feel that the salary or conditions do not match your expectations, now is the time to renegotiate. If you are experienced and well qualified you are in a strong position, provided you do not make a high salary your only objective. Find out what salary and conditions other companies offer for a similar position. Often a good strategy is to accept the salary offered for the first six months only. Ask if it would be possible to negotiate a rise after this initial period and once you have proved yourself.

During the negotiation, pay attention to the language and non-verbals so that you can apply the NLP techniques to create rapport. Emphasize your strengths and stay calm and focused. If your request is turned down you need to weigh up the pros and cons to see if the offer is acceptable. Take all the factors into consideration and do your research. Sometimes taking a job at a lower salary can lead to other opportunities that may not have been obvious at the time. A point to bear in mind is that employers are more likely to be interested in you when you are working for another company! You will gain valuable experience and then in a couple of years you might be in a stronger position to negotiate.

So, if after all you have decided you are in a position to negotiate, you will need to consider what to say and how to say it.

In order to be assertive without aggression, follow these tips:

▶ Take different points of view on the chin and allow that people have varied opinions – do you need to be right or do you want to be respected?

▶ Other people have needs and desires that we cannot always meet – that's OK.

▶ Maintain a firm and steady voice when faced with aggression or persuasion.

▶ Stand firm and keep eye contact initially (look away to disengage).

▶ Breathe deeply at least twice before answering any comments.

▶ Use positive language that shows the other person respect (even if they do not show it to you – model who you are).

▶ Do not take any comments personally.

▶ Allow any disruptive or aggressive remarks to 'blow' past you.

When you are in a discussion that involves standing up for your views, you need to speak with conviction. You need strong evidence to back up your facts. This is where your company research is invaluable.

If you want people to take action use active speech and back it up with evidence.

For example: 'I feel strongly that *you should consider giving me* a bonus as our department has had consistently high sales this year.'

If, however, it is someone else who needs to take action you use passive speech.

For example: 'This is vital to the business going forward. In my view *staff need to be persuaded* to accept the changes.'

Here are a few useful phrases you can try when putting forward strong views:

- It is my firm belief that...

- I hear what others are saying, however it is my strong desire to...

- If we look at the clear facts of this case we can see that...

- Not only is there... but also...

- It is out of the question to assume that...

- I am absolutely convinced that...

- I urge you to...

- Urgent action needs to be taken...

- People's jobs are at risk unless we take action.

- I am sure you agree that...

- Research tells us that...

- In my opinion...

- This is what we need to do, right now...

- Unless we take action on this today, orders will be delayed.

Finally, you need to consider the actions that you want your employer to take as a result of your negotiation. Perhaps all you need is for them to listen, take in the facts and reflect on the information. Whatever you decide, clarity is key. Ask yourself what result you want and what, if anything, your employer should be doing or acting on.

Final considerations

It is always easier to work towards your goal with others than to work alone. If you have colleagues in the same position, why not form a group to support and model each other? Use the group to hone your skills in the key areas you need for your interview. I suggest you meet regularly every six weeks to support each other and discuss how to stay motivated. If you feel the need for someone with experience and expertise, then hire a job or career coach as this can really help to support you. They can coach you individually or with your colleagues in a group to keep costs to a minimum.

I wish you the best of luck – go for it!

Key idea

On my first visit to Switzerland I felt hemmed in by the mountains surrounding me. It was only later, when I reached the mountain tops and learnt to ski down them, that I realized there was a whole new world opening up I had not seen before. Sometimes when we look up we fail to see the possibilities; the climb and effort seem insurmountable – but often just one step up is all that is needed to start a new journey.

Focus points

The main points to remember from this chapter are:

* Being too positive can hamper your progress.
* Rejection happens, and you can learn from it.
* Learn how to model success.
* If you are offered the job, be sure it meets your needs, or negotiate.
* It is easier to work towards your goal with others than to work alone.

Appendix: Additional exercises

Self-coaching questions for job hunters

Open questions are useful for self-coaching.

Rudyard Kipling wrote:

> I have six serving men
> They taught me all I knew
> Their names were 'What Why When, How Where and Who'

Here are a few questions for you to use in self-coaching:

1 What would I like to happen?

2 If I have a clear outcome/goal what would that be?

3 Anything else/What else? (Useful questions to repeat several times about your outcome)

4 What needs to happen for me to take the next step?

5 What kind of next step is that?

6 Is there anything else about that next step?

7 What might stop me?

8 How far is that true/Is that a belief?

9 What belief would I rather have?

10 If I were to do X what would the consequences be? (Possibly the positive opposite of what you said was stopping you)

11 What would that result in?

12 How do I keep myself motivated?

13 What needs to happen now?

14 What one action would make a difference?

15 What resources/skills/people do I need?

16 How can they support me?

17 What have I already got in place?

18 How can I find other alternative ways to explore/use this information?

19 What assumptions could I be making that might hold me back?

20 In what way are they valid, relevant, true?

21 What are the implications of this?

22 What positive steps have I taken/can I now take?

23 What mental and physical rehearsal have I done?

24 Have I covered X, Y?

25 What else needs to happen for me to take this forward?

26 What happens just before I feel prepared and ready?

27 What actions can I now commit to?

28 Who else will I need to involve?

29 How will I know when I have done all I can?

30 How will I measure my actions/success/results?

31 On a scale of 1–10 how prepared do I feel?

32 What would make that a 10 if it isn't already?

The GROW model

This model was originally created by Graham Alexander and further developed by Sir John Whitmore. Many people are familiar with this very simple structure of supporting people to go from identifying their goal to taking clear action.

GROW (Goals; Reality; Options; What) is an acronym used as a management tool for problem solving and development.

In coaching it is best used within a context of awareness and responsibility, and with the aim of increasing these two key qualities. Otherwise it is no more than a mechanical problem-solving tool and will not achieve optimum performance results. When going through these steps you may have no specific goal to start with, in which case looking at the Reality and Options may be better places to start.

Ask yourself open questions and use other coaching methods mentioned in this book to work through each phase. It is very useful to check out how willing you are to move forward and to take responsibility for your choices. You may like to let family or colleagues know what you have planned as a result of this exercise. This means you have some accountability for your actions. (We all need a nudge now and then!)

This is an outline of the model for you to work through alone or with a coach.

GOALS	Identify long or short term objectives
REALITY	Explore the current situation Support to find positive aspects
OPTIONS	Discuss choices,
WHAT	Establish what will be done, when? Who will do it, by when? Is there the will to do it?

Naturally not all self-coaching sessions will need a model but this can be a useful focus when a clear goal is identified.

David Kolb's learning circle

A well-known way of describing experiential learning takes the form of a circle.

The process begins with:

▶ **First** you carry out an action (or visualize and yourself taking that action) and then see the effect of the action on and in the situation.

▶ **Second** understand these effects in the situation, so that if the same action were taken in similar circumstances you could anticipate what would follow. (For example at a job interview)

- **Third** these observations and reflections are then brought together into a 'theory' from which new implications for action can be worked out (e.g. planning, preparation and practice)

- **Finally** to use the 'theory' as a guide to act in a new situation.

Concrete experience validates and tests abstract concepts or 'theories' via feedback from the situation. These steps are shown as a circular movement, although actually, these things may be occurring at the same time.

If we take the following as an example:

CONCRETE EXPERIENCE:
You have identified that you are having difficulty finding a job or facing an interview.

OBSERVATION AND REFLECTION:
You go through some of the techniques/actions in the book and notice what is happening and reflect on this for the next coaching session or for yourself.

FORMING ABSTRACT CONCEPTS:
You then form ideas, metaphors, thoughts and concepts around the areas you notice and bring these to the coaching session and/or to your own awareness.

TESTING IN NEW OR SIMILAR SITUATIONS:
You explore with your coach (or with the methods and strategies in this book) how to put these ideas and/or new concepts or behaviours into practice where appropriate.

The SDOC tool

This model can be used when you are considering your strengths and development areas.

- Write down your key strong characteristics and what you do well – be bold!

- Then follow this with development areas/behaviours or where you lack training or knowledge.

- What do you see as your opportunities in the job market and what threats or challenges do you face?

Use large flipchart paper and coloured pens, or draw a box in colour on your computer.

Strengths	Development Areas	Opportunities	Challenges

The goal sheet

YOUR GOAL FOR THE NEXT THREE MONTHS

1 Take a large piece of paper and some coloured pens – draw three large empty shapes almost covering the page.

2 At the top of the page write your goal in one sentence. Make it an inspiring goal which will really stretch and challenge you. Use descriptive words. 'I'd like to go for promotion' is not very inspiring!

3 Extend this as follows: 'I'd like to take over the role of X so that I could; this would enable me To.'

DESCRIPTION OF GOAL AS IF ALREADY ACHIEVED

Go forward three months write a clear, vivid, detailed description of your goal **as if already achieved**. Write this in the first large shape on your paper. Use bright, inspirational words, describe what you imagine you and others will see, hear and feel when you reach your goal.

WHAT IS THE CURRENT REALITY OF THIS GOAL?

Write a clear, honest description of the **current reality** of the goal, without any judgement or analysis. Write this in the second large shape. This is what you have done so far if anything.

ACTIONS ARISING

Record the actions and date by when you will carry them out in the third large shape on your page.

AFFIRMATIONS

Affirmations are positive, **present tense** statements of the desired outcome, written in the first-person (*I am, can, have, see, understand, realize, know etc*).

Write 3 affirmations related to your goal and desired outcome.

Affirmations are very powerful statements that can help coachees to get rid of negative assumptions and beliefs:

Examples: *'I am in my new role and it feels great to be leading the team'*

'I now have new challenges and feel the support of the management team'

'I can easily hold this position and am learning all the time'

Guided visualization

All athletes use visualisation to challenge themselves to greater heights. For example, you want to make a key presentation at interview but are daunted by the prospect.

Close your eyes and visualize the following:

▶ Walking into the interview, head held high and feeling confident

▶ Standing at the front of the room being prepared and rehearsed

- Delivering the presentation with confidence and in a clear voice

- Handling the questions that may arise with clarity and focus

- Taking any action points and comments with calmness

- Walking out of the room feeling the presentation was a success

Act this out either with a colleague or at home in front of your family. The more times you do this the easier it becomes. Plan, prepare and practise for the presentation as outlined in this book.

Making key decisions

Think of a small decision, for example, choosing what to wear at an interview or when to tackle a certain task. Then close your eyes and 'ask' yourself what you should do. Take some moments to explore with questions in this book such as 'What happens just before I decide?'; 'And when I decide, then what happens?'. When you are ready, ask:

- What was the first thing that came into my mind?

- What did that tell you?

- What would need to happen for you to trust and develop positive thoughts/actions around this decision?

Very often you tune out to your own inner wisdom and experience. This exercise needs to be done on a regular basis to change patterns of behaviour. You can ask yourself the same questions as above. It will raise your awareness of your inner self and recreate the ability to make decision formed from your own knowledge and experience.

THE TWO POSSIBILITIES

Another very powerful way to decide between two options is to imagine you have a ball in each hand, containing the two options you are trying to choose between. Or, you could actually choose two objects the same – that way you can feel them in your hands too.

Weigh the two balls in your hands and imagine which one is the heavier and less favourable option. Imagine which one is the lighter and therefore the one you may feel is easier. Trust in the way you are imagining the decisions and ask why one could be heavier than the other. What is this telling you about the task/situation?

To continue this exercise it may be useful to explore whether in fact the decision is really only between two options. It may be that these can be combined in some way or that one option can complement another.

The same exercise can then continue as follows:

▷ Place the two imaginary (or actual) balls on the floor at equal distance from each other (you can draw two balls on two separate pieces of paper if no balls are available)

▷ Walk between the two balls (options) and see if there is a way to combine them. Again notice which one is easier and that you are drawn to.

▷ By doing this exercise you can often experience a shift in thinking and it can be quite revealing. Encourage yourself to come to a decision by choosing one option or combining them.

▷ Of course if there are more than two options then this can be done by drawing the options as diagrams on a piece of paper and weighing them to 'feel' which is the heaviest/lightest and so on.

This method helps you to 'see' and 'feel' what is often stuck in your mind or jumbled in your thoughts.

Taking it further

Arnold, J. (2010) *Coaching Skills for Leaders in the Workplace* (Oxford: How To Books)

Cooper, L. (2008) *Business NLP for Dummies* (Chichester: John Wiley & Sons)

Elston, T. and Spohrer, K. (2009) *Using NLP to Enhance Behaviour and Learning: A Handbook for Teachers* (Continuum)

Grove, D. J. and Panzer, B. I. (1989) *Resolving Traumatic Memories: Metaphors and Symbols in Psychotherapy* (New York: Irvington Publishers, Inc.)

Innes, J. (2009) *The Interview Book* (Harlow: Pearson)

Luft, Joseph (1969) *Of Human Interaction* (National Press Books)

O'Connor, J. and Lages, A. (2004) *Coaching with NLP* (London: Element)

Revell, J. and Norman, S. (1997) *In Your Hands: NLP for Teaching and Learning* (Saffire Press)

Index